enVisionmath 2.

Volume 1B Topics 5-8

Authors

Randall I. Charles
Professor Emeritus
Department of Mathematics
San Jose State University
San Jose, California

Jennifer Bay-Williams
Professor of Mathematics Education
College of Education and Human
Development
University of Louisville
Louisville, Kentucky

Robert Q. Berry, III
Associate Professor of
Mathematics Education
Department of Curriculum,
Instruction and Special Education
University of Virginia
Charlottesville, Virginia

Janet H. Caldwell
Professor of Mathematics
Rowan University
Glassboro, New Jersey

Zachary Champagne
Assistant in Research
Florida Center for Research in Science,
Technology, Engineering, and
Mathematics (FCR-STEM)
Jacksonville, Florida

Juanita Copley
Professor Emerita, College of Education
University of Houston
Houston, Texas

Warren Crown
Professor Emeritus of Mathematics
Education
Graduate School of Education
Rutgers University
New Brunswick, New Jersey

Francis (Skip) Fennell
L. Stanley Bowlsbey Professor
of Education and Graduate and
Professional Studies
McDaniel College
Westminster, Maryland

Karen Karp
Professor of Mathematics Education
Department of Early Childhood and
Elementary Education
University of Louisville
Louisville, Kentucky

Stuart J. Murphy
Visual Learning Specialist
Boston, Massachusetts

Jane F. Schielack
Professor of Mathematics
Associate Dean for Assessment and
Pre K-12 Education, College of Science
Texas A&M University
College Station, Texas

Jennifer M. Suh
Associate Professor for
Mathematics Education
George Mason University
Fairfax, Virginia

Jonathan A. Wray
Mathematics Instructional Facilitator
Howard County Public Schools
Ellicott City, Maryland

SAVVAS
LEARNING COMPANY

Mathematicians

Roger Howe
Professor of Mathematics
Yale University
New Haven, Connecticut

Gary Lippman
Professor of Mathematics and
Computer Science
California State University, East Bay
Hayward, California

ELL Consultants

Janice R. Corona
Independent Education Consultant
Dallas, Texas

Jim Cummins
Professor
The University of Toronto
Toronto, Canada

Debbie Crisco
Math Coach
Beebe Public Schools
Beebe, Arkansas

Kathleen A. Cuff
Teacher
Kings Park Central School District
Kings Park, New York

Erika Doyle
Math and Science Coordinator
Richland School District
Richland, Washington

Reviewers

Susan Jarvis
Math and Science Curriculum Coordinator
Ocean Springs Schools
Ocean Springs, Mississippi

ISBN-13: 978-0-328-93067-8
ISBN-10:   0-328-93067-9

6   22

Subtract Within 100 Using Strategies

Essential Question: What are strategies for subtracting numbers to 100?

Digital Resources

Solve   Learn   Glossary

Tools   Assessment   Help   Games

Look at the big pieces of ice in the water!

How can heating and cooling change water and ice?

Wow! Let's do this project and learn more.

Math and Science Project: Heating, Cooling, and Subtraction

Find Out Have an adult help you heat and cool water and other materials. Find out if water and ice can change back and forth. Find out if heating and cooling an egg can change it back and forth.

Journal: Make a Book Show what you learn in a book. In your book, also:

• Tell about how heating and cooling are related.

• Tell about how addition and subtraction are related.

Name _____

Review What You Know

A-Z Vocabulary

1. Circle each **difference** in the math problems shown below.

$$15 - 5 = 10$$

```
  23        14
+ 32       - 7
----       ----
  55         7
```

2. Circle the statement if it describes **mental math**.

Math that is done with paper and pencil.

Math that you can do in your head.

3. Circle the statement if it describes **compatible numbers**.

Numbers that are close to numbers that you want to add or subtract.

Numbers that you can add or subtract using mental math.

Addition and Subtraction Facts

4. Complete the related addition and subtraction facts below.

$$6 + \boxed{} = 13$$

$$13 - \boxed{} = 6$$

You can use addition facts to help you subtract.

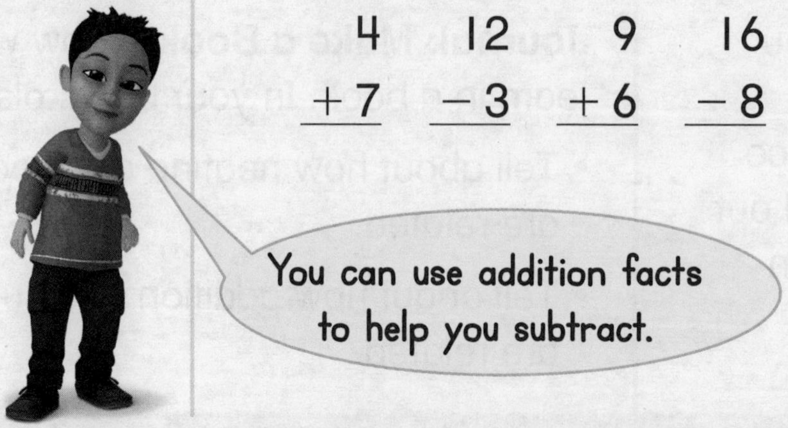

5. Write each sum or difference.

```
  4        12        9        16
+ 7       - 3      + 6      - 8
```

Math Story

6. Tim has 25 stamps. Roy gives him 51 more stamps. How many stamps does Tim have now?

_____ stamps

Solve & Share

How can you use the hundred chart to help you find 57 − 23? Explain. Write an equation.

Lesson 5-1
Subtract Tens and Ones on a Hundred Chart

I can ...
use a hundred chart to subtract tens and ones.

I can also make sense of problems.

1	2	3	4	5	6	7	8	9	10
11	12	13	14	15	16	17	18	19	20
21	22	23	24	25	26	27	28	29	30
31	32	33	34	35	36	37	38	39	40
41	42	43	44	45	46	47	48	49	50
51	52	53	54	55	56	57	58	59	60
61	62	63	64	65	66	67	68	69	70
71	72	73	74	75	76	77	78	79	80
81	82	83	84	85	86	87	88	89	90
91	92	93	94	95	96	97	98	99	100

_____ ◯ _____ = _____

Find 43 − 28 using a hundred chart.

I need to find the difference between 28 and 43.

Start at 28. Count to the next number that matches the ones in 43.

21	22	23	24	25	26	27	28	29	30
31	32	33	34	35	36	37	38	39	40
41	42	43	44	45	46	47	48	49	50

Count by ones! I counted 5 ones to get from 28 to 33.

Count by tens to 43.

21	22	23	24	25	26	27	28	29	30
31	32	33	34	35	36	37	38	39	40
41	42	43	44	45	46	47	48	49	50

That's 1 ten, or 10 more.

I added 5 and 10. That makes 15.

28 + 15 = 43
So, 43 − 28 = 15.

Do You Understand?

Show Me! How can you use a hundred chart to find 60 − 18?

☆ Guided Practice ☆

Subtract using the hundred chart. Draw arrows if you need to.

21	22	23	24	25	26	27	28	29	30
31	32	33	34	35	36	37	38	39	40
41	42	43	44	45	46	47	48	49	50
51	52	53	54	55	56	57	58	59	60
61	62	63	64	65	66	67	68	69	70

1. 69 − 36 = _33_

2. 54 − 24 = _____

3. _____ = 65 − 34

4. 47 − 22 = _____

Name _____

Tools   Assessment

Independent Practice   Subtract using the hundred chart. Draw arrows if you need to.

1	2	3	4	5	6	7	8	9	10
11	12	13	14	15	16	17	18	19	20
21	22	23	24	25	26	27	28	29	30
31	32	33	34	35	36	37	38	39	40
41	42	43	44	45	46	47	48	49	50
51	52	53	54	55	56	57	58	59	60
61	62	63	64	65	66	67	68	69	70
71	72	73	74	75	76	77	78	79	80
81	82	83	84	85	86	87	88	89	90
91	92	93	94	95	96	97	98	99	100

5. $54 - 7 = $ _____

6. _____ $= 96 - 63$

7. $45 - 22 = $ _____

8. $82 - 61 = $ _____

9. $65 - 21 = $ _____

10. _____ $= 79 - 47$

11. $84 - 6 = $ _____

Algebra Write the digit that makes each equation true.

12. $73 - \boxed{}2 = 41$

$5\boxed{} - 32 = 26$

13. $46 - \boxed{}1 = 15$

$78 - 36 = \boxed{}2$

14. $53 - \boxed{}2 = 31$

$99 - \boxed{}3 = 16$

Problem Solving

Use Tools Use the hundred chart to solve the problems below.

15. Darren's puzzle has 98 pieces. Darren fits 55 pieces together. How many more pieces does Darren still need to fit to complete the puzzle?

    _____ − _____ = _____ pieces

16. A test has 86 questions. Glenda needs to answer 23 more questions to finish the test. How many test questions has Glenda answered already?

    _____ questions

The hundred chart is a good tool to use. Count by ones and tens to subtract.

41	42	43	44	45	46	47	48	49	50
51	52	53	54	55	56	57	58	59	60
61	62	63	64	65	66	67	68	69	70
71	72	73	74	75	76	77	78	79	80
81	82	83	84	85	86	87	88	89	90
91	92	93	94	95	96	97	98	99	100

17. **Higher Order Thinking** Chris wants to subtract 76 − 42. Write the steps he can take to subtract 42 from 76 on the hundred chart.

    _____

    _____

    _____

18. ✓ **Assessment** Lu has 75 buttons. 49 of the buttons are green. The rest of the buttons are red. How many of the buttons are red?

    Ⓐ 16   Ⓑ 20   Ⓒ 26   Ⓓ 36

Name _____

 Help   Tools   Games

Another Look! Here is another way to subtract on a hundred chart.

Find 36 − 24.

1. Start at 36.

2. Move up 2 rows to subtract
   __2__ tens.

3. Move left 4 columns to subtract
   __4__ ones.

So 36 − 24 = 12.

1	2	3	4	5	6	7	8	9	10
11	12	13	14	15	16	17	18	19	20
21	22	23	24	25	26	27	28	29	30
31	32	33	34	35	36	37	38	39	40
41	42	43	44	45	46	47	48	49	50
51	52	53	54	55	56	57	58	59	60
61	62	63	64	65	66	67	68	69	70
71	72	73	74	75	76	77	78	79	80
81	82	83	84	85	86	87	88	89	90
91	92	93	94	95	96	97	98	99	100

HOME ACTIVITY Ask your child to subtract 58 − 23 on a hundred chart and explain how he or she subtracted.

Subtract using the hundred chart.

1. 87 − 7 = _____

2. 79 − 48 = _____

3. 65 − 41 = _____

4. 99 − 52 = _____

5. 35 − 13 = _____

6. _____ = 84 − 33

Algebra Write the digits that make each equation true.

7. $\boxed{}3 - 2\boxed{} = 71$ | 8. $5\boxed{} - \boxed{}1 = 14$ | 9. $78 - \boxed{}5 = 4\boxed{}$

10. **Look for Patterns** A treasure is hidden under one of the rocks. Follow the clues to find the treasure. Color each rock you land on.

1	2	3	4	5	6	7	8	9	10
11	12	13	14	15	16	17	18	19	20
21	22	23	24	25	26	27	28	29	30
31	32	33	34	35	36	37	38	39	40
41	42	43	44	45	46	47	48	49	50
51	52	53	54	55	56	57	58	59	60
61	62	63	64	65	66	67	68	69	70
71	72	73	74	75	76	77	78	79	80
81	82	83	84	85	86	87	88	89	90
91	92	93	94	95	96	97	98	99	100

A. Start at 55.   B. Subtract 20.

C. Add 5.   D. Add 20.

E. Add 10.   F. Subtract 5.

G. Subtract 20.   H. Add 5.

I. Subtract 20.   J. Subtract 5.

The treasure is hidden under the last rock that you colored. What is the number of that rock? _____ Describe the pattern you see in the numbers you colored.

11. **✓Assessment** A pan holds 36 biscuits. Kiana put 12 biscuits on the pan. How many more biscuits will fit on the pan?

Ⓐ 24   Ⓑ 23   Ⓒ 22   Ⓓ 21

12. **✓Assessment** A garden has room for 22 flowers. Dan needs to plant 11 more flowers to fill the garden. How many flowers did Dan already plant?

Ⓐ 10   Ⓑ 11   Ⓒ 12   Ⓓ 13

Name _____

Solve & Share

Jesse had 50 balloons at the fair.
A strong wind blew away 30 balloons.
How many balloons does Jesse have left?
Use the number line below to show your work.

I can ...
use an open number line to subtract tens.

I can also reason about math.

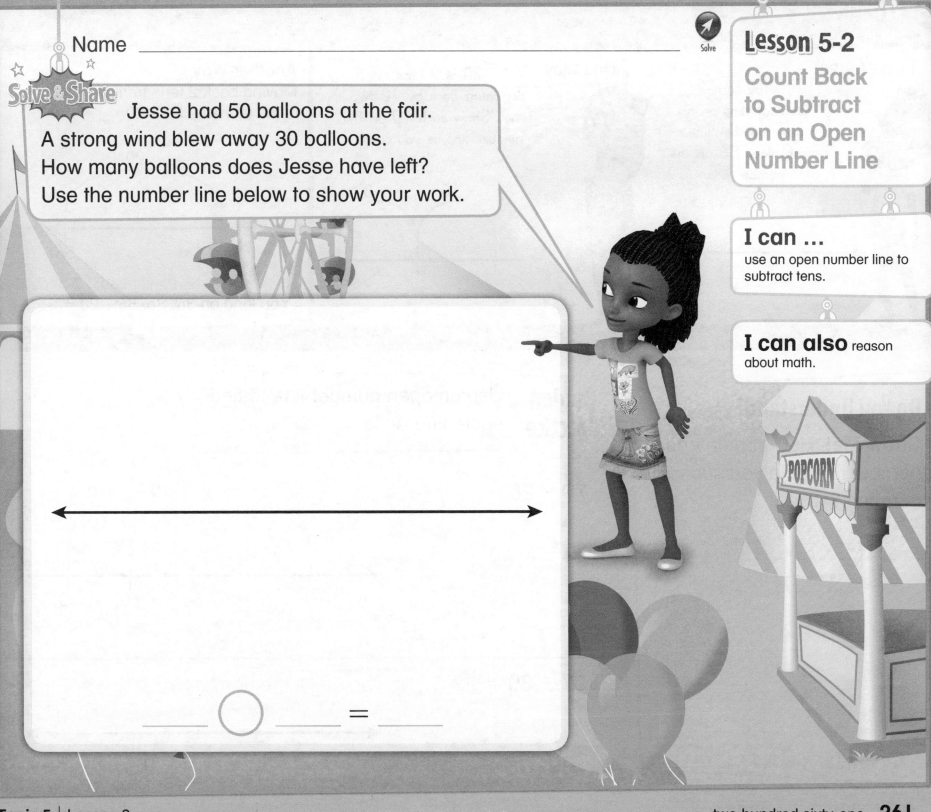

_____ ◯ _____ = _____

Find 56 − 20.

You can subtract tens on an open number line. First, place 56 on the number line.

56

One Way

20 is 2 tens. So, count back by 10 two times. Show each 10 on the number line as you count.

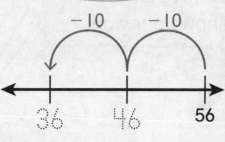

−10 −10

36 46 56

Another Way
Moving back 2 tens from 56 is the same as 56 − 20.

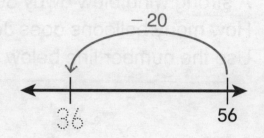

−20

36   56

You land on 36. So, 56 − 20 = __36__.

Do You Understand?

Show Me! How can an open number line help you subtract numbers?

⭐ **Guided Practice** ⭐ Use an open number line to find each difference.

1. 70 − 20 = _____

−10   −10

50   60   70

2. 67 − 30 = _____

Name _____

Independent Practice ☆ Use an open number line to find each difference.

3. 60 − 40 = _____

4. 85 − 20 = _____

5. 99 − 40 = _____

6. 42 − 30 = _____

7. 34 − 10 = _____

The number you are subtracting from should be put on the right side of the line.

8. Higher Order Thinking Jada drew this number line to find 79 − 40. She circled her answer. Did Jada get the correct answer? Explain.

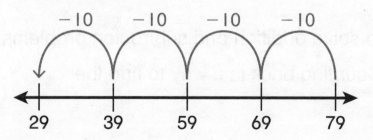

−10   −10   −10   −10

29   39   59   69   79

9. **Reasoning** Evan has 62 baseball cards. He gives 30 cards to Bridget. How many cards does Evan have left?

_____ baseball cards

10. **Math and Science** 45 icicles hang from a roof. 20 icicles melt and fall. How many icicles are left?

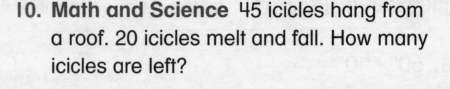

_____ icicles

11. **A-Z Vocabulary** Complete each sentence using one of the terms below.

    sum   **open number line**   **difference**

You can use an _____

_____ to solve addition and subtracton problems. Counting back is a way to find the

_____.

The _____ is the answer to an addition problem.

12. ✓ **Assessment** Which does the number line show? Choose all that apply.

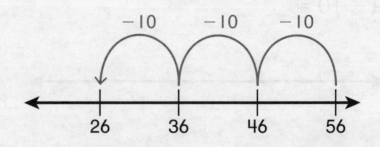

☐ Count back by 10 two times from 56.

☐ Count back by 10 three times from 56.

☐ $56 - 30 = 26$

☐ $26 + 56 = 82$

   Topic 5 | Lesson 2

Name _____

Help Tools Games

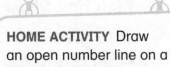

Another Look! Find 45 − 20 using an open number line.

You can use an open number line to make subtracting tens easier.

Place 45 on the number line. Then count back by 10 twice to subtract 20.

-10 $\quad$ -10

25   35   45

So, 45 − 20 = 25.

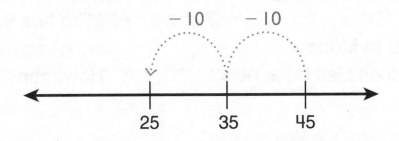

HOME ACTIVITY Draw an open number line on a sheet of paper. Then have your child find 33 − 20 using the number line.

Use an open number line to find each difference.

1. 30 − 20 = _____

2. 95 − 30 = _____

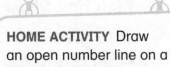

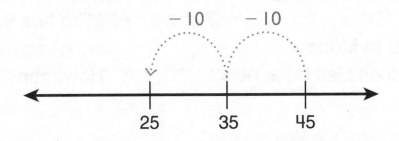

Use Tools Use an open number line to solve each problem.

3. $21 - 20 =$ _____

4. $15 - 10 =$ _____

5. Lisa has 25 beads.
She gives 10 beads to Maria.
How many beads does Lisa have now?

_____ beads

6. Mike has 43 balloons.
He gives away 20 balloons.
How many balloons does Mike have left?

_____ balloons

7. Higher Order Thinking Jackson drew this number line to solve a subtraction problem. Write the equation he solved.

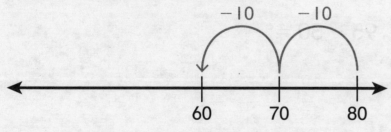

_____ – _____ = _____

8. ✓**Assessment** Which does the number line show? Choose all that apply.

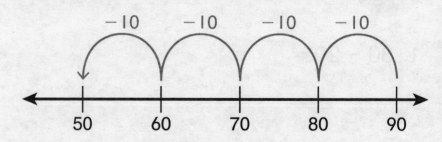

☐ Count back 4 tens from 90.

☐ Count back 40 from 90.

☐ $90 - 30 = 60$

☐ $90 - 40 = 50$

Name _____

Solve & Share

Jeremy had 56 bug stickers.
He gave 24 stickers to Eric.
How many bug stickers does Jeremy have left?
Use the open number line below to show your work.

Lesson 5-3

Continue to Count Back to Subtract on an Open Number Line

I can … use an open number line to subtract tens and ones.

I can also model with math.

_____ − _____ = _____

Name _____

Solve & Share

Jeremy had 56 bug stickers.
He gave 24 stickers to Eric.
How many bug stickers does Jeremy have left?
Use the open number line below to show your work.

_____ − _____ = _____

Lesson 5-3

Continue to Count Back to Subtract on an Open Number Line

I can … use an open number line to subtract tens and ones.

I can also model with math.

Topic 5 | Lesson 3   Digital Resources at SavvasRealize.com   two hundred sixty-seven **267**

Find 68 − 23.

Let's use an open number line and count back. First, place 68 on the line.

68

One Way
23 is 2 tens and 3 ones.
So, count back 2 tens from 68.
58, 48
Then, count back 3 ones from 48.
47, 46, 45

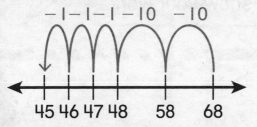

−1−1−1 −10 −10

45 46 47 48   58   68

Another Way
You can subtract 68 − 20 = 48,
then 48 − 3 = 45.

−3   −20

45 48   68

So, 68 − 23 = __45__.

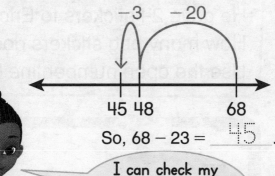

I can check my subtraction by adding 45 + 23 = 68.

Do You Understand?

Show Me! How can the open number line help you keep track as you count back?

☆ **Guided Practice** ☆ Use an open number line to find each difference.

1. 28 − 24 = _____

−4   −10   −10

4   8   18   28

2. 50 − 35 = _____

Name _____

Independent Practice ✰ Use an open number line to find each difference.

3. 45 − 13 = _____

4. 63 − 22 = _____

5. 78 − 46 = _____

6. 92 − 37 = _____

7. 80 − 44 = ?

> Break apart the number you are subtracting into tens and ones.

_____ − _____ = _____

8. Number Sense How many tens and ones will you count back to solve this problem: 56 − 38 = ? Solve the problem.

_____ tens _____ ones

_____ − _____ = _____

9. **Use Tools** There are 47 raffle tickets to sell for the fair. Ms. Brown's class sells 23 raffle tickets. How many raffle tickets are left to sell?

_____ raffle tickets

10. **Use Tools** Ethan counts 78 carrots. He sells 35 carrots at the farmers market. How many carrots does Ethan have left?

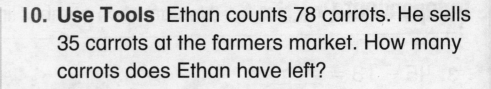

_____ carrots

11. **Higher Order Thinking** Show two different ways to find 63 – 25 using the open number lines.

63 – 25 = _____

12. **Assessment** Jen solved a subtraction problem using the open number line shown. Write the equation that her work below shows.

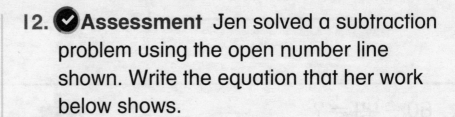

_____ – _____ = _____

Name _____

Another Look! Find $83 - 35$.

35

3 tens   5 ones

How many tens and ones do you need to subtract?

First place 83 on an open number line. Then count back 3 tens and 5 ones to subtract 35.

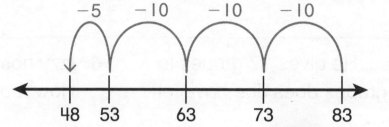

-5 -10 -10 -10

48   53   63   73   83

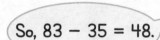
So, $83 - 35 = 48$.

HOME ACTIVITY Tell your child a subtraction story for $36 - 15$. Have your child draw an open number line and use it to solve the problem.

Use an open number line to find each difference.

1. $95 - 23 =$ _____

2. $30 - 15 =$ _____

Use Tools Use an open number line to solve each problem.

3. 87 − 23 = _____

4. 54 − 19 = _____

5. Joe has 43 grapes. He gives 17 grapes to Dee. How many grapes does Joe have left?

_____ grapes

6. Izzy has 99 bottle caps. She gives 33 to Max. How many bottle caps does Izzy have left?

_____ bottle caps

7. **Higher Order Thinking** Write a story problem for 36 − 14. Draw and use an open number line to solve the problem.

8. ✔**Assessment** Manuel solved a subtraction problem using the open number line shown. Write the equation his open number line shows.

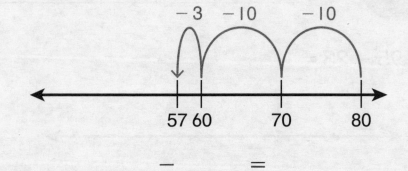

_____ − _____ = _____

Name _____

Solve & Share

There are 50 children at the park. 28 are boys and the rest are girls. How many girls are at the park?

Use the open number line to solve. Show your work.

I can ...
add up to subtract using an open number line.

I can also use math tools correctly.

←————————————————————————————→

_____ ◯ _____ = _____

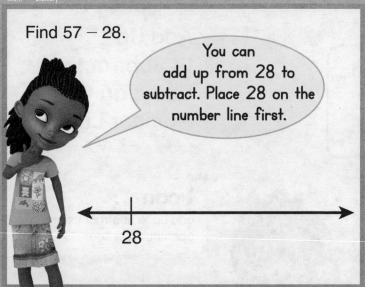

Find 57 − 28.

You can add up from 28 to subtract. Place 28 on the number line first.

28

You can add 2 to get to 30.

Then add 10, and 10 again, to get to 50.

Then add 7 to land on 57.

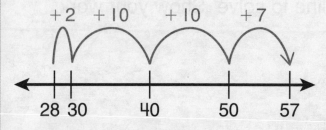

+2   +10   +10   +7

28 30   40   50   57

Add the tens and ones.

$2 + 10 + 10 + 7 = 29$

So, $57 − 28 = 29$.

I can check by adding!
$28 + 29 = 57$

Do You Understand?

Show Me! How can you add up to find 42 − 17?

☆ Guided Practice ☆

Add up to find each difference. Use an open number line.

1. 45 − 27 = _____

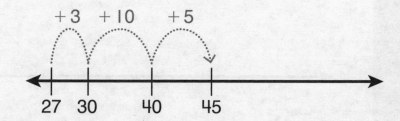

+3   +10   +5

27 30   40   45

2. 66 − 39 = _____

Independent Practice Add up to find each difference.
Use an open number line.

3. 41 − 19 = _____

4. 63 − 34 = _____

5. 83 − 58 = _____

6. 74 − 46 = _____

7. 72 − 34 = _____

Don't forget to find the sum of the tens and the ones you added up. That is the difference.

8. **Math and Science** Rob had 34 snowballs.
Some melted and now he has 18 snowballs.
How many snowballs melted?

_____ − _____ = _____

Add up to solve each problem. Use an open number line. Write the equations.

9. **Be Precise** Dino has 41 crayons. He gives 23 crayons to Bridget, and 7 crayons to Dan. How many crayons does Dino have left? Solve using two steps.

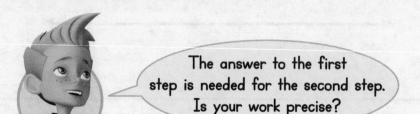

The answer to the first step is needed for the second step. Is your work precise?

Step 1: _____ ◯ _____ = _____

Step 2: _____ ◯ _____ = _____

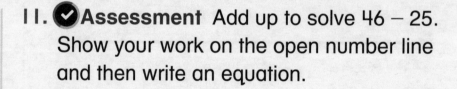

10. **Higher Order Thinking** Show two different ways to add up to find 72 − 35.

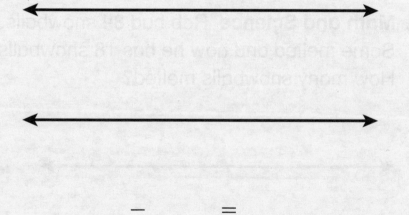

_____ − _____ = _____

11. ✅**Assessment** Add up to solve 46 − 25. Show your work on the open number line and then write an equation.

_____ − _____ = _____

Name _____

Another Look!

You can add up on an open number line to subtract 73 − 45.

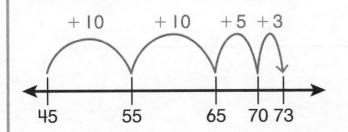

$$+10 \quad +10 \quad +5 \quad +3$$

45   55   65   70 73

So, 73 − 45 = 28.

You can start at 45. Add 10, and 10 again, to get to 65. Then add 5 to get to 70. Then add 3 to get to 73.

Add tens and ones to find the difference:

$$\underline{10} + \underline{10} + \underline{5} + \underline{3} = \underline{28}$$

HOME ACTIVITY Have your child tell a story about 52 − 34. Tell your child to solve the problem by adding up on an open number line. Then, have your child write an equation to show the answer.

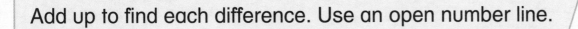
Add up to find each difference. Use an open number line.

1. 93 − 65 = _____

2. 84 − 67 = _____

Add up to solve each problem. Use an open number line. Write the equations.

3. **Use Tools** Misha has 36 bows. She gives 19 bows to Alice. How many bows does Misha have left?

_____ – _____ = _____

4. **Use Tools** Remi has 80 golf balls. He hits 53 of them. How many golf balls does Remi have left?

_____ – _____ = _____

5. **Higher Order Thinking** Richard found 93 – 67 by adding up on the open number line. Is he correct? Explain. Then write an addition equation to show how you could check his work.

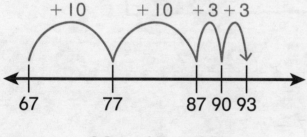

$$93 - 67 = 26$$

_____ ◯ _____ = _____

6. ✅ **Assessment** Use the open number lines. Show two different ways to add up to find 91 – 56.

One way

Another way

$$91 - 56 = \underline{\hspace{1cm}}$$

Topic 5 | Lesson 4

Name _____

Don wants to find 42 − 7 by breaking apart the 7 into two numbers. Use and draw place-value blocks to show how Don could find the difference.

I can ...
break apart 1-digit numbers to help me subtract mentally.

I can also break apart problems.

Digital Resources at SavvasRealize.com

$33 - 6 = ?$

You can break apart the number you are subtracting to find the difference.

Here are 3 ways to break apart 6. Which is best for subtracting 6 from 33?

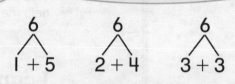

6
1 + 5

6
2 + 4

6
3 + 3

$33 - 6 = \underline{}$?

3   3

Start at 33. Subtract 3 to get to 30. Then subtract 3 more.

11	12	13	14	15	16	17	18	19	20
21	22	23	24	25	26	27	28	29	30
31	32	33	34	35	36	37	38	39	40

$33 - 6 = \underline{27}$

Do You Understand?

Show Me! Look at the problem above. Why wasn't the 6 broken apart into $1 + 5$ to find $33 - 6$?

☆ **Guided Practice** ☆ Subtract. Break apart the number you are subtracting. Show your work.

1. $43 - 9 = \underline{}$

2. $\underline{} = 24 - 6$

11	12	13	14	15	16	17	18	19	20
21	22	23	24	25	26	27	28	29	30
31	32	33	34	35	36	37	38	39	40
41	42	43	44	45	46	47	48	49	50

Name _____

Independent Practice Subtract. Break apart the number you are subtracting. Show your work. Use a hundred chart if needed.

3. $35 - 8 =$ _____

□   □

4. $41 - 5 =$ _____

□   □

5. _____ $= 82 - 7$

□   □

6. $53 - 7 =$ _____

□   □

7. $97 - 8 =$ _____

□   □

8. $64 - 9 =$ _____

□   □

9. $86 - 8 =$ _____

10. _____ $= 32 - 9$

11. $93 - 6 =$ _____

12. **Algebra** One number makes both equations true. Find the missing number.

$48 + \boxed{} = 56$ $56 - \boxed{} = 48$

The missing number is _____.

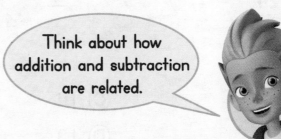

Think about how addition and subtraction are related.

13. **Explain** Karen has 7 pencils. Karen's teacher has 45 pencils. How many fewer pencils does Karen have than her teacher? Explain how you solved the problem.

_____

_____

_____

Is your explanation clear?

_____ fewer pencils

14. **Higher Order Thinking** Write a story problem about 63 − 8. Then solve.

_____

_____

_____

_____

$63 - 8 = $ _____

15. ✓**Assessment** Duane has 24 seashells. He gives 9 shells to his cousin Rob. How many seashells does Duane have now?

24 − 9 = ?

Ⓐ 16   Ⓒ 14

Ⓑ 15   Ⓓ 13

Help   Tools   Games

Another Look! Find 55 − 8.

You can break apart 8 to find 55 − 8.

One way is 8 = 5 + 3.

There is a 5 in the ones place in 55. It's easy to subtract 55 − 5.

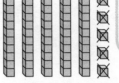

$$55 - 5 = 50$$

Next, subtract 50 − 3. You can count back 3 from 50.

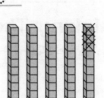

$$50 - 3 = 47$$

So, 55 − 8 = __47__.

HOME ACTIVITY Ask your child to show you how to break apart the 5 in 43 − 5 to find the difference.

Subtract. Break apart the number you are subtracting. Show your work.

1. 65 − 9 = _____

2. 24 − 7 = _____

3. _____ = 84 − 8

Explain Subtract. Break apart the number you are subtracting. Show your work to explain your thinking.

4. $41 - 5 =$ _____

5. _____ $= 94 - 8$

6. $25 - 9 =$ _____

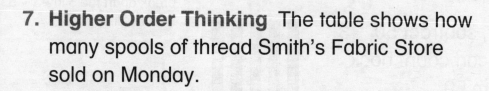

7. **Higher Order Thinking** The table shows how many spools of thread Smith's Fabric Store sold on Monday.

Before the sale, there were 34 red spools and 53 black spools. How many red spools were left at the end of Monday? How many black spools were left?

_____ red spools   _____ black spools

Spools of Thread Sold	
Thread Color	Number of Spools
Red	8
Blue	7
Black	6

8. ✓**Assessment** Ron has 21 comic books. He sells 6 of them to a friend. How many comic books does Ron have now?

Ⓐ 17   Ⓒ 15

Ⓑ 16   Ⓓ 14

9. ✓**Assessment** Yelena has 5 animal stickers. Vera has 41 animal stickers. How many fewer animal stickers does Yelena have than Vera?

Ⓐ 26   Ⓒ 35

Ⓑ 34   Ⓓ 36

Name _____

Solve

Lesson 5-6
Continue to
Break Apart
Numbers to
Subtract

Solve & Share

Gina wants to find 53 − 28 by breaking apart 28 into two numbers. Use place-value blocks and the hundred chart to show how Gina could find the difference.

I can …
break apart 2-digit numbers to help me subtract.

I can also break apart problems.

21	22	23	24	25	26	27	28	29	30
31	32	33	34	35	36	37	38	39	40
41	42	43	44	45	46	47	48	49	50
51	52	53	54	55	56	57	58	59	60
61	62	63	64	65	66	67	68	69	70

81 − 27 = ?

You can use place value to break apart the number you are subtracting.

Break apart 27 into tens and ones. Then break apart the ones.

27
20 + 7
        1 + 6

81 − 27 = _____ ?

20   7

1   6

Start at 81.
Subtract 20 to get to 61.
Then subtract 1 to get to 60.
Then subtract 6 more.

51	52	53	54	55	56	57	58	59	60
61	62	63	64	65	66	67	68	69	70
71	72	73	74	75	76	77	78	79	80
81	82	83	84	85	86	87	88	89	90

So, 81 − 27 = 54.

Do You Understand?

Show Me! How do you decide how to break apart the ones?

Guided Practice

Subtract. Break apart the number you are subtracting. Show your work.

1. 54 − 26 = _____

2. 43 − 18 = _____

21	22	23	24	25	26	27	28	29	30
31	32	33	34	35	36	37	38	39	40
41	42	43	44	45	46	47	48	49	50
51	52	53	54	55	56	57	58	59	60

Name _____

Independent Practice

Subtract. Break apart the number you are subtracting. Show your work. Use a hundred chart if needed.

3. _____ = 32 − 13

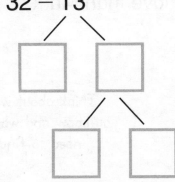

4. 74 − 28 = _____

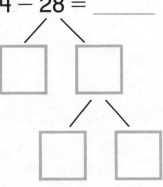

5. _____ = 61 − 47

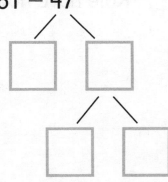

6. 84 − 46 = _____

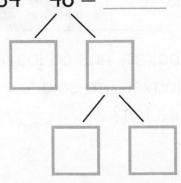

7. 46 − 17 = _____

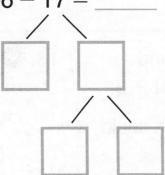

8. _____ = 95 − 38

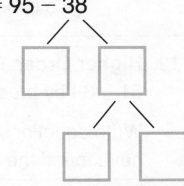

9. **Higher Order Thinking** Tina found 53 − 27 by breaking apart 27 into 23 and 4. Does Tina's way work?

Show another way you could break apart 27 to find 53 − 27. Then find the difference.

10. **Math and Science** Kate had 32 ice cubes. She put 14 of them in the sun and they melted. How many ice cubes does Kate have now?

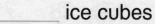 ice cubes

11. **Make Sense** Mark has 27 stamps. Sam has 82 stamps. Lena has 42 stamps. How many more stamps does Sam have than Mark?

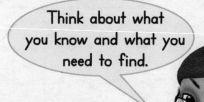

Think about what you know and what you need to find.

_____ more stamps

12. **Higher Order Thinking** Allison found 51 − 34 by breaking apart 34 into 31 + 3.

Write equations to show how Allison could have found the difference.

13. ✓**Assessment** A bakery has 66 loaves of bread. 27 of the loaves are sold. How many loaves are left?

(A) 39

(B) 38

(C) 37

(D) 36

Name _____

Help   Tools   Games

Another Look! Find 43 − 27.

To find 43 − 27, you can break apart 27.

One way is 20 + 7.

It's easy to find 43 − 20.

$$43 - 20 = 23$$

Next, subtract 23 − 7. You can break apart 7 into 3 + 4.

$$23 - 3 = 20 \text{ and}$$

$$20 - 4 = 16$$

So, 43 − 27 = 16.

Continue to Break Apart Numbers to Subtract

HOME ACTIVITY Ask your child to show you how to break apart 38 to find 65 − 38.

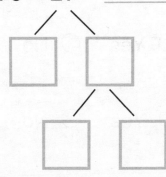

Subtract. Break apart the number you are subtracting. Show your work to explain your thinking.

1. 76 − 29 = _____

2. _____ = 82 − 39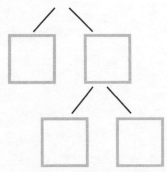

3. 92 − 16 = _____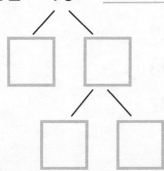

Explain Subtract. Break apart the number you are subtracting. Show your work. Be ready to explain why your way works.

4. $75 - 27 =$ _____

5. _____ $= 61 - 34$

6. $87 - 28 =$ _____

7. **Higher Order Thinking** Brian found $42 - 19$ by breaking apart 19 into $12 + 7$. Write equations to show how Brian could have found the difference.

How can place value help you solve the problem?

8. ✓**Assessment** Rosita has 55 grapes. She gives a friend 26 of her grapes. How many grapes does Rosita have now?

(A) 17

(B) 29

(C) 28

(D) 37

9. ✓**Assessment** Can you use the equations to find $86 - 27$? Choose Yes or No.

$86 - 20 = 66$ ○ Yes   ○ No
$66 - 7 = 59$

$26 - 10 = 16$ ○ Yes   ○ No
$16 - 6 = 10$

$86 - 20 = 66$ ○ Yes   ○ No
$66 - 6 = 60$
$60 - 1 = 59$

Name _____

Solve & Share

Yuri found 86 − 29 using mental math.

He changed 29 so it would be easier to find the difference.

Show how Yuri could have found the difference.
Explain how he could have used mental math.

I can …
make numbers that are easier to subtract, then use mental math to find the difference.

I can also break apart problems.

Learn Glossary

43 − 18 = ?

You can use compensation to make numbers that are easier to subtract.

It is easier to subtract 20, than 18.

One Way Add 2 to both numbers. Then subtract using mental math.

$$43 \quad - \quad 18 \quad = \quad ?$$
$$\downarrow +2 \qquad \downarrow +2$$
$$45 \quad - \quad 20 \quad = \quad 25$$

So, 43 − 18 = 25.

Another Way Add 2 to 18. Then subtract using mental math. Then add 2 to find the answer.

$$43 \quad - \quad 18 \quad = \quad ?$$
$$\qquad\qquad \downarrow +2$$
$$43 \quad - \quad 20 \quad = \quad 23$$
$$\qquad\qquad\qquad\qquad \downarrow +2$$

So, 43 − 18 = 25.

I subtracted 2 more than 18, so I need to add 2 to 23 to find the answer.

Do You Understand?

Show Me! Marc says to find 61 − 13, it's easier to subtract 10 instead of 13. He says if you subtract 3 from 13 to get 10, you must subtract 3 more from your answer. Do you agree? Explain.

☆**Guided Practice**☆ Use compensation to make numbers that are easier to subtract. Then solve. Show your work.

1. $52 \quad - \quad 8 \quad = \underline{\quad}$

$\downarrow$ +2 $\downarrow$ +2

$54 \quad - \quad 10 \quad = \quad 44$

2. $76 \quad - \quad 27 \quad = \underline{\quad}$

$\downarrow \Box \qquad \downarrow \Box$

$\underline{\quad} \quad - \quad \underline{\quad} \quad = \underline{\quad}$

3. $52 - 15 = \underline{\quad}$

$\downarrow$ +5

$52 \quad - \quad 20 \quad = \quad 32 \quad \cdots\rightarrow 37$

+5

4. $93 \quad - \quad 39 \quad = \underline{\quad}$

$\downarrow \Box$

$\underline{\quad} \bigcirc \underline{\quad} \quad = \underline{\quad} \rightarrow 54$

$\Box$

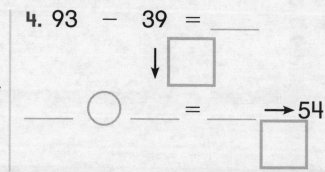

Tools   Assessment

Independent Practice

Use compensation to make numbers that are easier to subtract. Then solve. Show your work.

5. 73 – 9 = _____

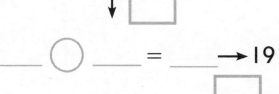

_____ ◯ _____ = _____ ⟶ 64

6. 35 – 16 = _____

_____ ◯ _____ = _____ ⟶ 19

7. 43 – 28 = _____

_____ ◯ _____ = _____ ⟶ 15

8. 51 – 27 = _____

_____ – _____ = _____

9. 74 – 35 = _____

_____ – _____ = _____

10. 99 – 21 = _____

_____ – _____ = _____

11. **Higher Order Thinking** Yoshi says that to find 91 – 32, she can subtract 2 from both numbers. Then subtract using mental math. She says the answer is 59. Do you agree?

Problem Solving ☆ Solve each problem. Show your thinking.

12. Make Sense There were some buttons in a jar. Mrs. Kim puts 19 more buttons in the same jar. Now there are 45 buttons in the jar. How many buttons were in the jar to begin with?

_____ buttons

13. Romi has 42 cards. Lisa has 75 cards. How many more cards does Lisa have than Romi?

_____ more cards

Think about what you are trying to find.

14. Higher Order Thinking Greg found 72 − 24. First he subtracted 20 because he thinks it is easier. Use words and numbers to explain how Greg could have found the difference.

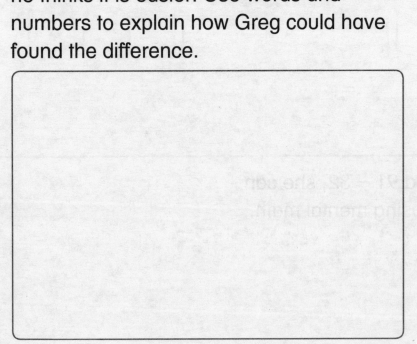

15. ✓ Assessment Use the numbers on the cards. Write the missing numbers to solve the problem.

| 2 | 25 | 30 | 55 |

$$53 \quad - \quad 28 \quad = \quad \underline{\hspace{2em}}$$

$$+ \ 2 \qquad + \ \boxed{}$$

$$\underline{\hspace{3em}} \quad - \quad \underline{\hspace{2em}} \quad = \quad \underline{\hspace{2em}}$$

Name _____

Help Tools Games

Homework & Practice 5-7
Subtract Using Compensation

Another Look! You can use compensation to find $64 - 27$.

27 is close to __30__ .

$27 + $ __3__ $ = $ __30__

It's easy to find $64 - 30$.

$64 - 27 = ?$

     $\downarrow + 3$

$64 - 30 = 34 \rightarrow 37$

         $+ 3$

So, $64 - 27 = $ __37__ .

Since I subtracted 30, I subtracted 3 more than 27.

So, I need to add 3 to 34 to find the answer.

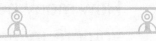

HOME ACTIVITY Ask your child to show you how to use compensation to find $82 - 49$.

Use compensation to make numbers that are easier to subtract. Then solve. Show your thinking.

1.

$65 - 48 = $ ___

     $\downarrow$ ☐

___ ◯ ___ $ = $ ___ $\rightarrow 17$

☐

2.

$96 - 37 = $ ___

     $\downarrow$ ☐

___ ◯ ___ $ = $ ___ $\rightarrow 59$

☐

3.

$24 - 18 = $ ___

     $\downarrow$ ☐

___ ◯ ___ $ = $ ___ $\rightarrow 6$

☐

Topic 5 | Lesson 7   Digital Resources at SavvasRealize.com   two hundred ninety-five **295**

Solve each problem. Show your work.

4. Make Sense A store had 45 hats for sale. On Friday, 26 of the hats were still for sale. How many hats sold? Think about what you are trying to find.

_____ hats

5. (A-Z) Vocabulary Complete each sentence using one of the terms below.

regroup   subtract

To find $56 + 38$, you can _____ 14 ones as 1 ten and 4 ones.

You can use compensation to help you add and _____ mentally.

6. Higher Order Thinking Use compensation to find $93 - 78$. Use words, pictures, or numbers to explain how you found the difference.

7. ✓Assessment Use the numbers on the cards. Write the missing numbers to solve the problem.

| 2 | 29 | 31 | 50 |

$81 - 52 =$ _____
$\downarrow -2$

$81 \bigcirc \square = \square \rightarrow \square$
$\square$

Solve & Share

Some frogs were sitting on a pond.
16 more frogs joined them.
Now there are 49 frogs on the pond.
How many frogs were on the pond at first?
Show how you know.

I can ...
solve one- and two-step problems using addition or subtraction.

I can also use math tools correctly.

_____ frogs

Brian had some baseball cards. Eric gave Brian 6 more cards. Now Brian has 15 cards. How many baseball cards did Brian have at first?

You can use a model to keep track of the numbers.

You know the whole and one part.

15

? | 6

You can use addition or subtraction to solve the problem.

$\underline{9} + 6 = 15$

or

$15 - 6 = \underline{9}$

So, Brian had $\underline{9}$ cards at first.

Check that your answer makes sense.

Brian had 9 cards. Then Eric gave him 6 more cards. Now he has 15 cards.

$9 + 6 = 15$

My answer makes sense!

Do You Understand?

Show Me! Cory scored some points. Then he scored 8 more points. He scored 14 points in all. How many points did Cory score at first? How can you solve the problem?

☆ **Guided Practice** ☆ Complete both equations to solve the problem. Use the model to help you.

1. Some people got on the bus at the first stop.
   9 more people got on the bus at the second stop.
   There are 21 people on the bus now.
   How many people got on the bus at the first stop?

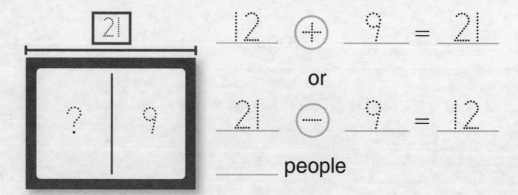

21

? | 9

$\underline{12} \oplus \underline{9} = \underline{21}$

or

$\underline{21} \ominus \underline{9} = \underline{12}$

_____ people

Independent Practice ☆ Solve each problem. Show your work.

2. Mr. Wing's class collected some cans to recycle
on Tuesday. They collected 18 more cans on
Wednesday. The class collected 44 cans in all.
How many cans did the class collect on Tuesday?

You can use
addition or subtraction
to solve this problem.

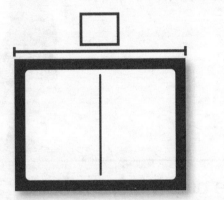

_____ + _____ = _____

or

_____ – _____ = _____

_____ cans

3. Sue took out 5 books from the library on
Monday. She took out 6 books from the library
on Tuesday. Then she returned 3 books on
Wednesday. How many books does Sue have
on Thursday?

_____ books

4. **Higher Order Thinking** There are 24 peas on Kim's plate.
Kim eats 15 peas. Then Kim's mother puts 8 more peas on
her plate. How many peas are on Kim's plate now?

Step 1

_____ – _____ = _____

Step 2

_____ + _____ = _____   _____ peas

Think about what you know and what you are trying to find.

5. **Make Sense** Elaine put 13 photos in the album. Ken put some more photos in the album. There are 32 photos in the album in all. How many photos did Ken add?

_____ photos

6. **Make Sense** Kris sees some students in the library. Then 10 more students enter the library. Now Kris sees 20 students in the library. How many students were in the library in the beginning?

_____ students

7. **Higher Order Thinking** There are 15 vocabulary words in Week 1. There are 8 more vocabulary words in Week 2 than in Week 1.

How many words are there in both weeks?

Step 1: _____ + _____ = _____

Step 2: _____ + _____ = _____

_____ words

8. ✓**Assessment** Blake puts 8 marbles in the bag. Cole puts 9 marbles in the bag. Then Blake takes out 7 marbles from the bag. How many marbles are in the bag now?

Solve. Show your work in the table.

Step 1
Step 2
Answer: _____ marbles

Name _____

Another Look! You can solve a two-step problem by writing two equations.

Rena counts 6 birds in the tree. 3 birds fly away. Then 8 more birds land in the tree. How many birds does Rena count in the tree now?

Step 1
Subtract to find how many birds are in the tree after 3 birds fly away.

Step 2
Add the number of birds that landed in the tree.

HOME ACTIVITY Make up a two-step story problem for your child to solve.

$$6 - 3 = 3$$

$$3 + 8 = 11$$

_____ birds

Complete both equations to solve each problem.

1. Lucy collects 9 rocks. She gives 4 rocks to Sam. Then Lucy collects 7 more rocks. How many rocks does Lucy have now?

   _____ rocks

   Step 1:
   _____ − _____ = _____

   Step 2:
   _____ + _____ = _____

2. 4 boys ride their bicycles to the park. 6 more boys ride their bicycles to the park. Then 2 boys go home. How many boys are at the park now?

   _____ boys

   Step 1:
   _____ + _____ = _____

   Step 2:
   _____ − _____ = _____

Solve each problem. Show your work.

3. **Model** Michael put some of the dishes away. Scott put 17 dishes away. They put away 32 dishes in all. Use the bar diagram to model the story. Then write 2 equations the model shows. How many dishes did Michael put away?

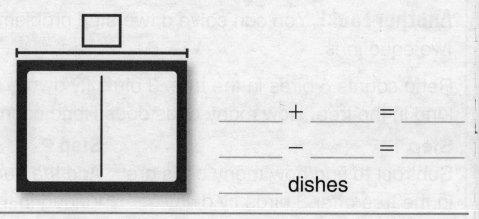

_____ + _____ = _____

_____ − _____ = _____

_____ dishes

4. **Higher Order Thinking** Kina picked 14 green apples. Her dad picked 8 red apples. Then they each ate 2 apples. How many apples do they have now? Explain how you solved the problem.

_____

_____

_____

_____

_____

_____

_____ apples

5. ✓ **Assessment** 3 black cats were in the alley. 5 cats joined them. Then 6 cats walked away. How many cats are still in the alley?

Solve. Show your work in the table.

Step 1
Step 2
Answer: _____ cats

Name _____

Solve & Share

Bill collects and sells seashells. He has 45 shells, finds 29 shells, and sells 20 shells. How many seashells does Bill have now?

Tara says you have to subtract 45 − 29 and then add 20 to solve the problem. Do you agree with Tara's thinking? Circle your answer. Use pictures, words, or equations to explain.

I can ...
critique the thinking of others by using what I know about addition and subtraction.

I can also add and subtract two-digit numbers.

Agree   **Do Not Agree**

Thinking Habits
What questions can I ask to understand other people's thinking?

Are there mistakes in other people's thinking?

42 people are swimming. Some people leave. Now 15 people are swimming.

Kelly added up to subtract and she says 17 people left.

How can I decide if I agree with Kelly?

I can check for mistakes or ask Kelly questions.

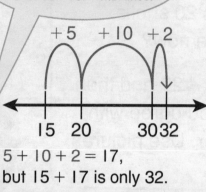

I can draw a number line and add up to check for mistakes.

+5 +10 +2

15 20   30 32

$5 + 10 + 2 = 17$,
but $15 + 17$ is only 32.

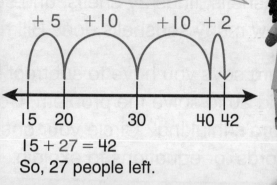

Kelly's strategy of adding up is good, but her answer is not correct.

+5 +10   +10 +2

15 20   30   40 42

$15 + 27 = 42$
So, 27 people left.

Do You Understand?

Show Me! What question would you ask Kelly to help her check her reasoning?

☆ Guided ☆ Practice

Circle the answer. Use pictures, words, or equations to explain your reasoning.

1. 51 people were on a train. 33 people left the train. How many people are on the train now?

   Ryan says 18 people. He broke apart 33 into 30 and 3. Then he subtracted each number. Does Ryan's reasoning make sense?

   Agree   **Do Not Agree**

   _____

   _____

   _____

   _____

   _____

Tools   Assessment

Independent Practice

Circle the answer. Use pictures, words, or equations to explain your reasoning.

2. Jill put 53 buttons in a box. Marci put 17 buttons in another box.

   Jarod says Marci has 33 fewer buttons than Jill. He thinks 53 − 20 is easier to subtract than 53 − 17. He subtracts 53 − 20 and gets 33.

   Do you agree or not agree with Jarod's thinking?

   Agree   **Do Not Agree**

3. Rob has 68 more puzzle pieces than Gina. Rob has 90 puzzle pieces.

   Carol says Gina has 22 puzzle pieces. Carol says she found 90 − 68 using an open number line. She added up 2 and 20 more from 68 and got 90.

   Does Carol's reasoning make sense?

   Agree   **Do Not Agree**

Problem Solving

Reading Books

Ricky read the first 3 chapters of a book. Chapter 1 has 11 pages. Chapter 2 has 7 pages. Chapter 3 has 9 pages.

Sally read 46 pages of her book. How many more pages did Sally read than Ricky?

4. Make Sense What steps do you need to take to solve the problem?

_____

_____

_____

5. Look for a Pattern Is there a shortcut to find how many pages Ricky read? Explain.

_____

_____

_____

_____

6. Explain Sally drew this open number line. Sally says she read 21 more pages than Ricky. Do you agree? Explain.

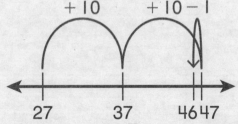

_____

_____

_____

_____

_____

Name _____

Help   Tools   Games

Homework & Practice 5-9
Critique Reasoning

Another Look!

Shane has 62 stamps. Jake has 36 stamps.

Nita says Jake has 26 fewer stamps than Shane, because she can break apart 36 and subtract $62 - 30 = 32$ and $32 - 6 = 26$. Is Nita correct?

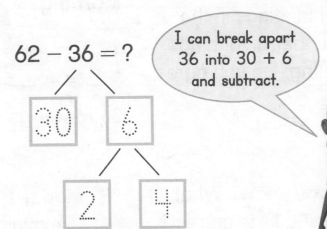

$62 - 36 = ?$

I can break apart 36 into $30 + 6$ and subtract.

$62 - 30 = 32$
$32 - 2 = 30$ and $30 - 4 = 26$
So, $62 - 36 = 26$.
Yes, Nita is correct.

HOME ACTIVITY Take turns writing your own subtraction problems involving two-digit numbers. Make some mistakes in some of your solutions. Then challenge each other to find the mistakes.

Circle the answer. Use pictures, words, or equations to explain.

1. There were 64 runners in a race last year. This year there were 25 fewer runners.

Latoya says 39 runners were in the race this year. She says $64 - 30$ is easy to subtract. So she added $25 + 5 = 30$. Then she found $64 - 30 = 34$, and added 5 to 34 to get 39.

Agree   **Do Not Agree**

Landing Planes

Luis says the number of landings in the afternoon equals the number of landings in the morning and evening. Do you agree with Luis?

Morning

36 landings

Afternoon

74 landings

Evening

38 landings

2. **Make Sense** What do you know? What do you need to do to tell if Luis is correct?

_____

_____

_____

_____

3. **Model** Use pictures, words, or equations to explain if Luis's thinking is correct.

_____

_____

_____

_____

4. **Explain** Luis got his answer by finding 74 − 38 = 36.

Do you agree with Luis's thinking? Use pictures, words, or equations to explain.

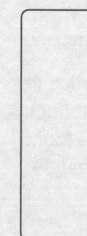

Name _____

Find a Match

Find a partner. Point to a clue. Read the clue.

Look below the clues to find a match. Write the clue letter in the box next to the match.

Find a match for every clue.

I can …
add and subtract within 20.

Clues

A Every difference is 10.

B Every sum is 11.

C Every sum and difference is 6.

D Exactly three sums are the same.

E Exactly three differences are the same.

F Every sum is the same as 9 + 4.

G Every difference is odd.

H Exactly three sums are even.

☐ 12 − 5 17 − 8 14 − 7 16 − 9	☐ 10 − 0 20 − 10 14 − 4 19 − 9	☐ 6 + 6 2 + 8 7 + 4 5 + 7	☐ 14 − 8 3 + 3 15 − 9 0 + 6
☐ 8 + 6 7 + 8 9 + 6 10 + 5	☐ 15 − 8 18 − 9 12 − 7 13 − 6	☐ 5 + 6 4 + 7 9 + 2 3 + 8	☐ 7 + 6 3 + 10 8 + 5 4 + 9

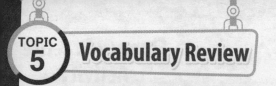

TOPIC 5 — Vocabulary Review

Glossary

Word List
- break apart
- compatible numbers
- compensation
- difference
- mental math
- ones
- open number line
- tens

Understand Vocabulary

Choose a term from the Word List to complete each sentence.

1. You can count back or add up to subtract on an

   _____.

2. To find $42 - 7$, you can _____ 7 into $2 + 5$.

3. The answer to a subtraction problem is called the _____.

4. There are 6 _____ in the number 36.

5. In 43, there are _____ tens.

6. In 76, there are _____ tens and _____ ones.

7. Break apart 8 to find $65 - 8$.

   _____

Use Vocabulary in Writing

8. Use words to tell how to find $54 - 19$. Use terms from the Word List.

   _____

   _____

   _____

   _____

   _____

Set A

You can use a hundred chart to help you subtract. Find 65 − 31.

Start at 31. Move right 4 ones to 35.
Then move down 3 tens to 65.
3 tens and 4 ones is 34.

So, 65 − 31 = _34_ .

31	32	33	34	35	36	37	38	39	40
41	42	43	44	45	46	47	48	49	50
51	52	53	54	55	56	57	58	59	60
61	62	63	64	65	66	67	68	69	70

Use a hundred chart to solve the problems.

Reteaching

1. 67 − 42 = _____

2. 70 − 33 = _____

3. 58 − 42 = _____

4. 63 − 38 = _____

Set B

You can use an open number line to find 85 − 30.

Place 85 on the number line.

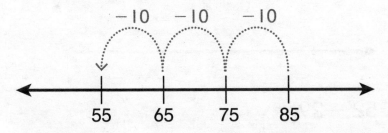

30 is 3 tens. Count back by 10 three times from 85.

So, 85 − 30 = _55_ .

Use an open number line to find each difference.

5. 60 − 20 = _____

6. 78 − 40 = _____

You can use an open number line to find $57 - 24$.

Place 57 on the number line. There are 2 tens in 24. So, count back by 10 two times. There are 4 ones in 24. Then count back 4 from 37.

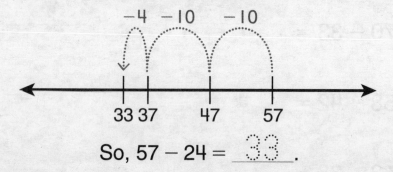

So, $57 - 24 = \underline{33}$.

Find $62 - 37$.

Place 37 on the line. Add 3 to get to 40. Then add two 10s to get to 60. Then add 2 to get to 62. Add the tens and ones: $3 + 10 + 10 + 2 = 25$.

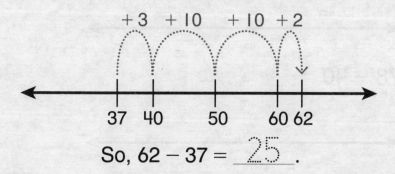

So, $62 - 37 = \underline{25}$.

Use an open number line to find each difference.

7. $38 - 13 = \underline{}$

8. $93 - 36 = \underline{}$

Add up on an open number line to find each difference.

9. $75 - 47 = \underline{}$

10. $52 - 29 = \underline{}$

Name _____

Set E

Break apart 17 to find 54 − 17.

21	22	23	24	25	26	27	28	29	30
31	32	33	34	35	36	37	38	39	40
41	42	43	44	45	46	47	48	49	50
51	52	53	54	55	56	57	58	59	60

54 − 17

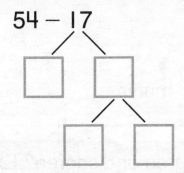

Start at 54. Subtract 10. Then subtract 4 to get to 40. Then subtract 3 more.

So, 54 − 17 = _37_.

Set F

74 − 27 = ?

Use compensation to solve.

$$74 - 27$$
$$\downarrow +3$$
$$74 - 30 = 44 \dashrightarrow 47$$
$$+3$$

So, 74 − 27 = _47_.

Subtract. Break apart the number you are subtracting. Show your work.

Reteaching
Continued

11. 52 − 23 = _____

12. 45 − 19 = _____

Use compensation to make numbers that are easier to subtract. Then solve.

13. 42 − 18 = _____

14. 84 − 37 = _____

Topic 5 | Reteaching

three hundred thirteen **313**

Mason reads 34 pages in two days. He reads 8 of the pages on the second day. How many pages does Mason read the first day?

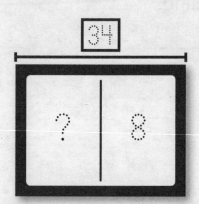

$26 + 8 = 34$ and
$34 - 8 = 26$

____26____ pages

Add or subtract to solve the problem. Show your work.

15. Gene bakes 60 muffins in one day. He bakes 24 of the muffins before lunch. How many muffins does he bake after lunch?

_____ ◯ _____ = _____

_____ muffins

Thinking Habits

Critique Reasoning

What questions can I ask to understand other people's thinking?

Are there mistakes in other people's thinking?

Do you agree or disagree? Explain.

16. Ken has 29 more stamps than Jamie. Ken has 52 stamps. Lisa says Jamie has 23 stamps.

Lisa added up 1 from 29, then 20 more from 30, and 2 more to get to 52. Does Lisa's reasoning make sense?

Name _____

1. A store has 68 candles. Then they sell 29 of the candles.
   How many candles are left?

   Ⓐ 29   Ⓑ 38   Ⓒ 39   Ⓓ 97

2. Which does the number line show? Choose all that apply.

   ☐ Count back by 10 two times from 48.

   ☐ Count back by 10 three times from 48.

   ☐ 48 − 30 = 18

   ☐ 18 + 48 = 66

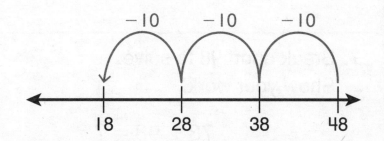

3. Tony has 66 rocks.
   He gives 23 rocks to Chris.

   How many rocks does Tony have now?

   _____ ◯ _____ = _____

   _____ rocks

21	22	23	24	25	26	27	28	29	30
31	32	33	34	35	36	37	38	39	40
41	42	43	44	45	46	47	48	49	50
51	52	53	54	55	56	57	58	59	60
61	62	63	64	65	66	67	68	69	70

4. Raven solved a subtraction problem
   using the number line. Write the equation
   that the number line shows.

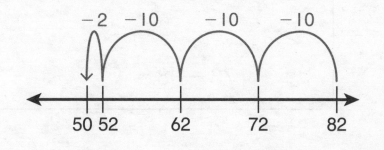

   _____ − _____ = _____

5. Ella has 7 carrots.
Ann has 34 carrots.
How many fewer carrots does
Ella have than Ann?

Ⓐ 7 Ⓒ 34

Ⓑ 27 Ⓓ 41

6. Keena has 64 balloons.
28 of the balloons are red.
14 balloons are green.
The rest of the balloons are purple.
How many of the balloons are purple?

Ⓐ 22 Ⓒ 42

Ⓑ 36 Ⓓ 50

7. Break apart 48 to solve.
Show your work.

$$73 - 48 = ?$$

$$73 - 48 = \underline{\hspace{2cm}}$$

8. Joe has 43 stickers.
Then he gives away 9 stickers.
How many stickers does Joe have left?

Can you use the two equations to solve?
Choose Yes or No.

$43 + 7 = 50$	◯ Yes	◯ No
$50 + 2 = 52$		
$43 + 10 = 53$	◯ Yes	◯ No
$53 - 1 = 52$		
$43 - 3 = 40$	◯ Yes	◯ No
$40 - 6 = 34$		
$43 - 10 = 33$	◯ Yes	◯ No
$33 + 1 = 34$		

Name _____

9. Which does the number line show? Choose all that apply.

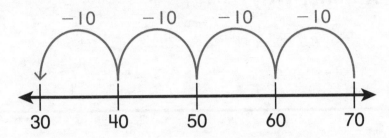

☐ Count back 4 tens from 70.

☐ Count back 4 from 70.

☐ $70 - 30 = 40$

☐ $70 - 40 = 30$

10. Use the open number line to find the difference.

$$80 - 42 = ?$$

$80 - 42 = $ _____

11. **Part A** 33 ants are on a leaf. 15 ants leave. How many ants are left?
Jay adds 2 to 33 to make an easier problem, 35–15. He says 20 ants are left. Circle whether you agree or do not agree.

Agree   **Do Not Agree**

Part B Explain why you agree or do not agree with Jay's strategy.

12. Use the open number lines. Show two different ways to find 74 − 28.
Show your work.

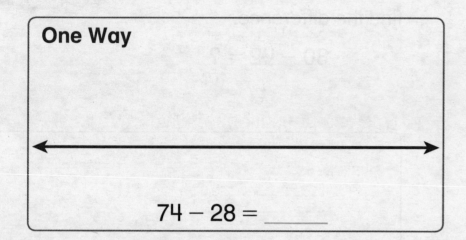

One Way

74 − 28 = _____

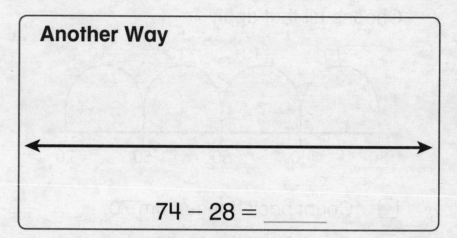

Another Way

74 − 28 = _____

13. Use the numbers on the cards.
Write the missing numbers to solve
the problem.

| 3 | 35 | 40 | 75 |

72 − 37 = _____

+3   ☐ +

_____ − _____ = _____

14. 5 black cows are at the ranch.
9 brown cows join them.
Then 6 cows leave the ranch.
How many cows are still at the ranch?

Solve. Show your work in the table.

Step 1	
Step 2	
Answer	
_____ cows	

Name _____

Beautiful Boats

Chen's family goes to the lake for a vacation.
They count the boats that they see.

12 sailboats   28 rowboats   36 motorboats

1. How many more motorboats does
   Chen see than sailboats?

   Use the open number line to
   solve.

_____ more motorboats

2. Maria's family saw 57 rowboats
   on their vacation. How many
   more rowboats did they see
   than Chen's family?

   Use compensation to solve.
   Explain how you found your answer.

   _____

   _____

   _____

   _____

   _____

   _____

                        _____ more rowboats

3. Chen's sisters play with toy boats at the lake. They have 21 yellow boats. They have 9 fewer red boats than yellow boats. How many boats do they have in all?

Write two equations to solve the problem.

_____ − _____ = _____

_____ + _____ = _____

_____ boats

4. Julie's family saw 94 boats on their vacation. How many more boats did they see than Chen's family?

Part A What do you need to do to solve the problem?

Part B How many boats did Chen see? Show your work. Then explain how you found your answer.

_____ boats

Part C Julie said that her family saw 18 more boats than Chen's family. She broke apart 76 into 70 + 4 + 2. Then she subtracted each number from 94. Does Julie's reasoning make sense? Explain.

Fluently Subtract Within 100

Essential Question: What are strategies for subtracting numbers to 100?

Digital Resources

Solve Learn Glossary

Tools Assessment Help Games

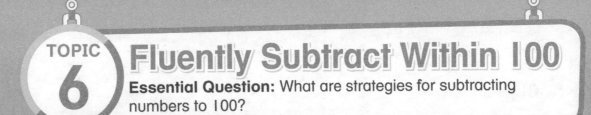

More of Earth is covered with water than with land!

And some of the land is covered with snow and ice!

Wow! Let's do this project and learn more.

Math and Science Project: Finding Water and Finding Differences

Find Out Use globes, maps, books, and other sources to find out where water, snow, and ice can be found on Earth. Make a list of different names of bodies of water and names of bodies of snow and ice.

Journal: Make a Book Show what you learn in a book. In your book, also:

- Tell about how globes are models that show where water is found on Earth.

- Tell about how to use a subtraction model to find differences.

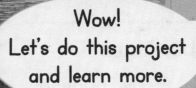

Name _____

Review What You Know

A-Z Vocabulary

1. **Break apart** 56 into tens and ones. Draw place value blocks to show the parts.

   56 = _____ + _____

2. Complete the drawing to show how to **regroup** 1 ten as ones.

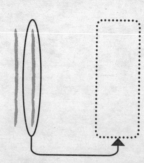

3. Complete the **bar diagram** to model $64 - 31 = ?$

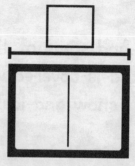

Open Number Lines

4. Find $40 - 25$ by counting back on an open number line. Show your work.

   $40 - 25 =$ _____

5. Find $45 - 22$ by adding up on an open number line. Show your work.

   $45 - 22 =$ _____

Math Story

6. Lea has 30 cookies. She gives 17 cookies to her friends. How many cookies does Lea have now?

   _____ cookies

Name _____

Solve & Share

How can you use tens and ones to find 23 − 6?
Use place-value blocks to help you. Show your work.

_____ − _____ = _____

Find 34 − 6. Show 34. There are not enough ones to subtract 6.

You need to regroup.

Regroup 1 ten as 10 ones.

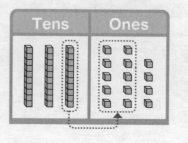

Subtract 6.

Cross out 6 ones to subtract. Now there are 2 tens and 8 ones left that show the difference.

$34 - 6 = \underline{28}$

Do You Understand?

Show Me! Do you need to regroup when you subtract 5 from 44? Explain why or why not.

☆ **Guided Practice** ☆ Subtract. Use your workmat and place-value blocks. Regroup if you need to.

	Show.	Subtract.	Do you need to regroup?		Find the difference.
1.	35	8	Yes	No	$35 - 8 = \underline{27}$
2.	46	3	Yes	No	$46 - 3 = \underline{}$
3.	62	4	Yes	No	$62 - 4 = \underline{}$
4.	50	7	Yes	No	$50 - 7 = \underline{}$

Tools   Assessment

Independent Practice

Subtract. Use your workmat and place-value blocks. Regroup if you need to.

	Show.	Subtract.	Do you need to regroup?		Find the difference.
5.	81	2	Yes	No	81 − 2 = _____
6.	29	1	Yes	No	29 − 1 = _____
7.	60	4	Yes	No	60 − 4 = _____
8.	24	9	Yes	No	24 − 9 = _____
9.	75	3	Yes	No	75 − 3 = _____
10.	43	5	Yes	No	43 − 5 = _____

11. **Higher Order Thinking** Which one-digit numbers can you subtract from 74 without first regrouping? Explain how you know.

Think about what each digit stands for in 74.

_____

_____

12. **Make Sense** There are 21 snails in a garden. 6 snails leave. How many snails are still in the garden?

_____ snails

13. **Make Sense** Kate has 45 marbles. She gives 3 marbles to her brother. How many marbles does Kate have now?

_____ marbles

14. **Higher Order Thinking** Sammie has 9 fewer rings than Emilio.
Sammie has 7 more rings than Sara.
Emilio has 34 rings.
Complete the sentences below.
Draw a picture to explain your work.

Sammie has _____ rings.

Sara has _____ rings.

15. ✓ **Assessment** Malcolm has 38 seeds. Juan has 4 fewer seeds than Malcolm. Juan gives 8 seeds to his friend. How many seeds does Juan have now?

Ⓐ 22

Ⓑ 26

Ⓒ 36

Ⓓ 46

Think about what you know and what you are trying to find. Can drawing place-value blocks help?

Another Look! Use place-value blocks to find 42 − 7.

Show 42.	Regroup.	Subtract 7 ones.
Tens / Ones	Tens / Ones	Tens / Ones

HOME ACTIVITY Ask your child to show you how to subtract 26 − 7 using small objects such as buttons, marbles, or paper clips. Have your child explain and show you how to regroup.

12 − 7 = ___5___ ones

42 − 7 = ___35___

Subtract. Use the pictures to help.

1. Subtract 5 from 31.

Show 31.	Regroup.	Subtract ___ ones.
Tens / Ones	Tens / Ones	Tens / Ones

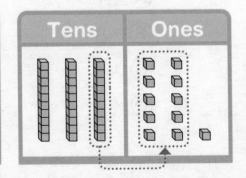

11 − 5 = _____ ones

31 − 5 = _____

2. 🅰🅩 **Vocabulary** Circle the missing word.

addend   **equation**

$42 - 7 = 35$ is an _____.

3. **Algebra** What number is missing?

_____ $- 5 = 20$

4. **Algebra** What number is missing?

$37 -$ _____ $= 28$

Make Sense Solve. Think about what you know and need to find.

5. Maria buys 36 beads.
She uses 9 of the beads.
How many beads does Maria have left?

_____ beads

6. Luke buys 7 new pencils.
Now he has 21 pencils.
How many pencils did Luke have at first?

_____ pencils

7. **Higher Order Thinking** A flag pole is 30 feet tall. A bug crawls 14 feet up the pole. Then it crawls another 4 feet up the pole. How much farther must the bug crawl to get to the top?

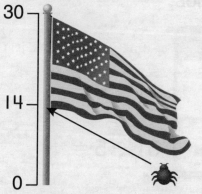

_____ feet

8. ✅ **Assessment** An old building has 48 big windows.
The building has 12 small windows.
There are 9 broken windows.
How many windows are **NOT** broken?

Ⓐ 51

Ⓑ 48

Ⓒ 41

Ⓓ 37

328 three hundred twenty-eight

Name _____

Solve & Share

There are 22 students drawing pictures.
4 students finish drawing. How many students are still drawing?

Use place-value blocks to help you solve.
Show the tens and ones you have.

I can ...
use place value and models to subtract 2-digit and 1-digit numbers.

I can also use math tools correctly.

Tens	Ones

_____ tens   _____ ones

$$22 - 4 = \_\_\_\_$$

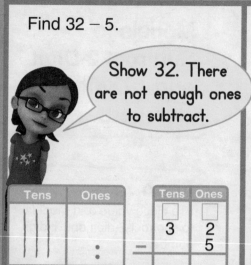

Find 32 – 5.

Show 32. There are not enough ones to subtract.

Tens	Ones
3	2
	5

Regroup 1 ten as 10 ones.

Write 2 to show 2 tens.
Write 12 to show 12 ones.

Tens	Ones
2 ~~3~~	12 ~~2~~
	5

Subtract the ones.
Then subtract the tens.

Tens	Ones
2 ~~3~~	12 ~~2~~
	5
2	7

There are 2 tens and 7 ones left.

So, 32 – 5 = __27__.

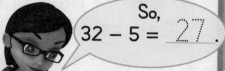

Tens	Ones
2 ~~3~~	12 ~~2~~
	5
2	7

Do You Understand?

Show Me! Why do you need to regroup when you subtract 32 – 5?

☆ **Guided Practice** ☆ Subtract. Draw place-value blocks to show your work. Regroup if needed.

1.

Tens	Ones
3 ~~4~~	14 ~~4~~
	9
3	5

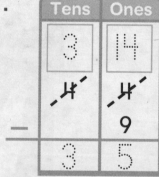

Tens	Ones

2.

Tens	Ones
2	3
	5

Tens	Ones

3.

Tens	Ones
3	5
	8

Tens	Ones

330 three hundred thirty

Topic 6 | Lesson 2

Tools Assessment

Independent Practice Subtract. Draw place-value blocks to show your work. Regroup if needed.

4.

Tens	Ones
☐	☐
6	3
−	2

Tens	Ones

5.

Tens	Ones
☐	☐
9	1
−	7

Tens	Ones

6.

Tens	Ones
☐	☐
6	6
−	9

Tens	Ones

7.

Tens	Ones
☐	☐
5	2
−	6

Tens	Ones

Write the missing numbers in the boxes. Draw a picture to show and explain your work.

8. Algebra What numbers will complete the subtraction equations?

$\boxed{} - 8 = 17$ $34 - \boxed{} = 29$

Problem Solving **Model** Solve the problems below. Draw place-value blocks to model.

---

9. There are 23 students playing tag. 9 students go home. How many students are still playing tag?

Tens	Ones

_____ students

---

10. There are 67 books on the shelf. Dion takes 5 of them. How many books are left on the shelf?

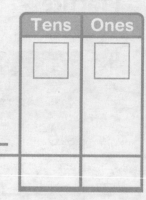

Tens	Ones

_____ books

---

11. **Higher Order Thinking** What mistake did Alia make when she subtracted 72 − 4? Show how to fix her mistake.

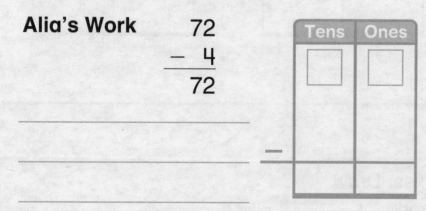

Alia's Work
```
   72
 −  4
   72
```

Tens	Ones

_____

_____

_____

---

12. ✅**Assessment** You draw place value blocks to model each subtraction. Would you regroup to show the difference? Choose Yes or No.

29 − 3 = ?   ◯ Yes   ◯ No

30 − 0 = ?   ◯ Yes   ◯ No

77 − 8 = ?   ◯ Yes   ◯ No

55 − 5 = ?   ◯ Yes   ◯ No

Help   Tools   Games

Another Look! Regroup when there are not enough ones. Find 52 − 8.

Step 1
Show 52. There are not enough ones to subtract 8.

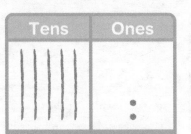

Tens	Ones
5	2
	8
−	

Step 2
Regroup 1 ten as 10 ones.

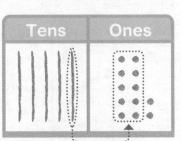

Tens	Ones
4	12
5̷	2̷
	8
−	

Step 3
Subtract the ones. Then subtract the tens.

Tens	Ones
4	12
5̷	2̷
	8
4	4

So, 52 − 8 = __44__.

HOME ACTIVITY Write 22 − 6 in vertical form on a piece of paper. Ask your child to show you how to find 22 − 6 using small objects such as paper clips, buttons, or marbles. Have your child write the difference.

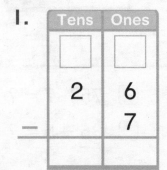

Subtract. Draw place-value blocks to show your work. Regroup if needed.

1.

Tens	Ones
2	6
	7
−	

Tens	Ones

2.

Tens	Ones
4	3
	9
−	

Tens	Ones

Model Solve each problem. Draw place-value blocks to model.

3. There are 40 students in the gym. 9 students are jumping rope. How many students are **NOT** jumping rope?

Tens	Ones
□	□
−	

_____ students

4. Kate writes on 7 pages in her notebook. There are 34 pages in her notebook. How many pages are blank?

Tens	Ones
□	□
−	

_____ pages

5. **Higher Order Thinking** Write a subtraction story about 45 − 8. Then solve.

_____

_____

_____

_____

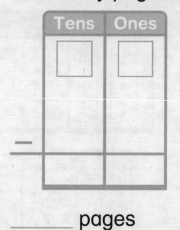

6. ✓**Assessment** You draw place value blocks to model each subtraction. Choose all of the problems that need regrouping to show the difference.

☐ 62 − 4 = ?   ☐ 75 − 7 = ?

☐ 58 − 7 = ?   ☐ 35 − 5 = ?

Name _____

Solve & Share

Ari has 31 stickers.
He puts 8 of his stickers in a scrapbook.
How many stickers are left?

Solve. Explain why your strategy works.

I can ...
use place value and regrouping to subtract.

I can also look for things that repeat.

Tens	Ones
−	

_____

_____

_____

_____

_____

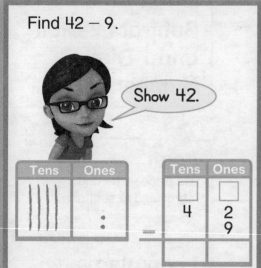

Find 42 − 9.

Show 42.

Tens	Ones
4	2
	9

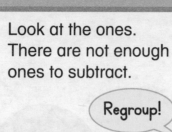

Look at the ones.
There are not enough
ones to subtract.

Regroup!

Tens	Ones
3 / 4	12 / 2
	9

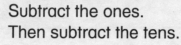

Subtract the ones.
Then subtract the tens.

Tens	Ones
3 / 4	12 / 2
	9
3	3

There are 3 tens
and 3 ones left.

42 − 9 = 33

Tens	Ones
3 / 4	12 / 2
	9
3	3

Do You Understand?

Show Me! Look at the
regrouping in the problem
above. Why is 12 written
above the 2 in the ones
column?

1.
Tens	Ones
2 / 3	16 / 6
	8
2	8

2.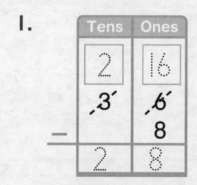
Tens	Ones
2	9
	4

3.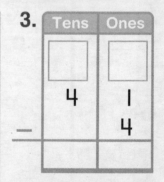
Tens	Ones
4	1
	4

4.
Tens	Ones
6	3
	5

5.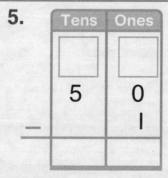
Tens	Ones
5	0
	1

6.
Tens	Ones
4	8
	7

Topic 6 | Lesson 3

Name _____

Independent Practice Subtract. Use drawings if needed.

7.
Tens	Ones
☐	☐
3	2
	6
−	

8.
Tens	Ones
☐	☐
2	0
	3
−	

9.
Tens	Ones
☐	☐
6	7
	6
−	

10.
Tens	Ones
☐	☐
5	2
	4
−	

11.
Tens	Ones
☐	☐
3	5
	0
−	

12.
Tens	Ones
☐	☐
7	5
	3
−	

13.
Tens	Ones
☐	☐
5	6
	7
−	

14.
Tens	Ones
☐	☐
8	5
	1
−	

15.
Tens	Ones
☐	☐
9	8
	9
−	

16.
Tens	Ones
☐	☐
7	7
	9
−	

Use words or a picture to solve.

17. Number Sense What is the missing number? Explain how to solve.

$45 - 9 = 46 - $ ☐

Problem Solving ✫ Solve the problems below.

18. Generalize There are 25 bikes at a bike store. The store owner sells 7 bikes. How many bikes are left?

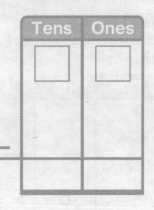

You can repeat steps to subtract. First subtract the ones. Regroup if needed. Then subtract the tens. 7 has zero tens.

_____ bikes

---

19. Higher Order Thinking A bike store sold 10 fewer locks on Wednesday than on Tuesday. How many more locks did the store sell on Wednesday than on Monday?

Bike Locks Sold	
Monday	9
Tuesday	33
Wednesday	

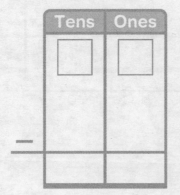

_____ locks

20. ✅ **Assessment** Use the numbers on the cards to find the missing numbers in the problem. Write the missing numbers.

| 15 | 9 | 3 |

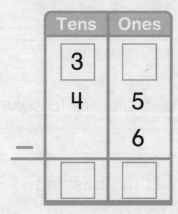

Think: How will I regroup to subtract?

 Topic 6 | Lesson 3

Name _____

Another Look! Find 42 − 6. You can subtract the ones first.

Think: Are there enough ones to subtract?

There are **NOT** enough ones to subtract.

Regroup if you need to. Then subtract the tens. Draw pictures if needed.

1-digit numbers have 0 tens.

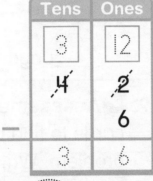

Tens	Ones
3	12
4̸	2̸
−	6
3	6

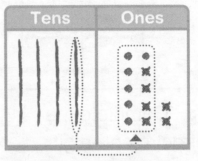

So, 42 − 6 = 36.

Regroup? (Yes)   No

HOME ACTIVITY Write 34 − 9 in vertical form on a sheet of paper. Have your child use pencil and paper to solve.

Subtract. Use drawings if needed.

1.

Tens	Ones
☐	☐
2	5
−	4

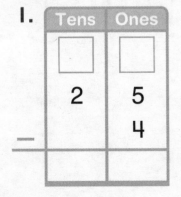

2.

Tens	Ones
☐	☐
4	1
−	8

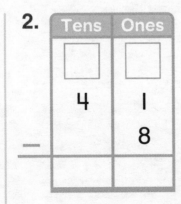

3.

Tens	Ones
☐	☐
6	5
−	7

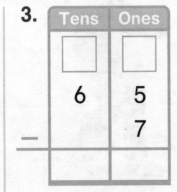

4.

Tens	Ones
☐	☐
7	8
−	9

5.

Tens	Ones
☐	☐
8	3
−	6

Generalize Solve the problems. Show your work and regroup if needed.

6. 53 grapes are on a plate. Andrea eats 5 of them. How many grapes are on the plate now?

Tens	Ones

_____ grapes

7. Chato reads 7 pages. His book has 67. How many pages does Chato have left to read?

Tens	Ones

_____ pages

8. **Higher Order Thinking** Complete the subtraction frame. Subtract a one-digit number from a 2-digit number.

Tens	Ones
7	6

You know the difference! Work backwards to check your work. There is more than one correct answer.

9. ✓ **Assessment** Use the numbers on the cards to find the missing numbers in the problem. Write the missing numbers.

1	8	11

Tens	Ones
2	1
1	

with the 3 in the ones column and the subtraction

Name _____

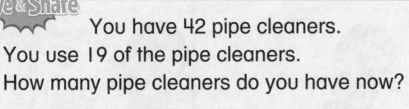

Solve & Share

You have 42 pipe cleaners.
You use 19 of the pipe cleaners.
How many pipe cleaners do you have now?

Use place-value blocks to help you solve.
Draw your place-value blocks.
Tell if you need to regroup.

I can ...
use place value and models to subtract 2-digit numbers.

I can also use math tools correctly.

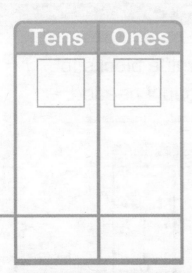

Tens	Ones

Regroup?

Yes   No

_____ pipe cleaners

Find 31 − 14.

Show 31. There are not enough ones to subtract.

Regroup 1 ten as 10 ones.

Write 2 to show 2 tens. Write 11 to show 11 ones.

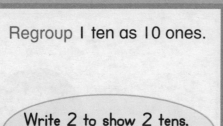

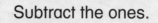

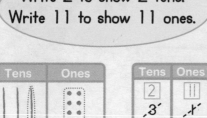

Subtract the ones.

Subtract the tens.

So, 31 − 14 = __17__.

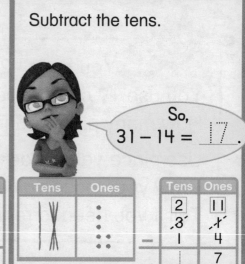

Do You Understand?

Show Me! Explain why you need to regroup to find 65 − 17.

⭐ **Guided Practice** ⭐ Subtract. Draw place-value blocks to show your work. Regroup if needed.

1.

Tens	Ones
4 12	
5̷	2̷
1	3
3	9

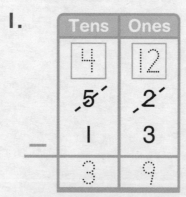

2.

Tens	Ones
4	1
2	6

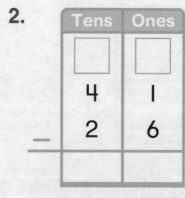

3.

Tens	Ones
6	4
4	7

Name _____

Tools Assessment

Independent Practice Subtract. Draw place-value blocks to show your work. Regroup if needed.

4.

Tens	Ones
☐	☐
5	6
− 3	1

Tens	Ones

5.

Tens	Ones
☐	☐
6	6
− 5	8

Tens	Ones

6.

Tens	Ones
☐	☐
8	5
− 4	6

Tens	Ones

7.

Tens	Ones
☐	☐
4	3
− 1	5

Tens	Ones

8. Algebra Write numbers to complete the equations. Draw pictures to help if needed.

$37 - 18 = \boxed{}$

$46 - \boxed{} = 18$

$\boxed{} - 17 = 16$

9. Number Sense
Do these models show the same value? Explain.

_____

_____

_____

10. **Model** Anita has $63. She spends $24 and saves the rest. How much does Anita save?

$_____

Tens	Ones

What kind of picture can you draw to model the subtraction?

11. **Higher Order Thinking** Write a subtraction story about 36 − 17. Explain how to solve the problem.

_____

_____

_____

_____

_____

_____

12. ✓**Assessment** Sara has 70 beads. There are 11 beads that are **NOT** round. The rest are round. How many round beads does Sara have?

Ⓐ 59

Ⓑ 49

Ⓒ 47

Ⓓ 11

Name _____

Help   Tools   Games

Homework & Practice 6-4

Models to Subtract 2-Digit Numbers

HOME ACTIVITY Ask your child to use paper clips or other small objects to find 25 – 16. Have your child explain how he or she regrouped.

Another Look! Find 43 – 16.

Step 1

Show 43. There are not enough ones to subtract 6.

Tens	Ones
││││	⋮

Tens	Ones
☐	☐
4	3
– 1	6

Step 2

Regroup 1 ten as 10 ones.

Tens	Ones
││││⊘	⋮⋮⋮⋮

Tens	Ones
3	13
4̸	3̸
– 1	6

Step 3

Subtract the ones. Then subtract the tens.

Tens	Ones
││⋊	••• ••× ••× ••×

Tens	Ones
3	13
4̸	3̸
– 1	6
2	7

So, 43 – 16 = 27 .

Subtract. Draw place-value blocks to show your work. Regroup if needed.

1.

Tens	Ones
☐	☐
5	0
– 1	3

Tens	Ones

2.

Tens	Ones
☐	☐
7	6
– 2	8

Tens	Ones

Topic 6 | Lesson 4

Digital Resources at SavvasRealize.com

three hundred forty-five **345**

Model Solve. Draw models to show your work.

3. Jamal has 54 marbles. Lucas has 70 marbles. How many more marbles does Lucas have than Jamal?

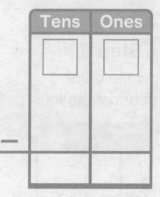

_____ more marbles

4. Latoya has 95 pennies. She gives 62 pennies to her cousin. How many pennies does Latoya have now?

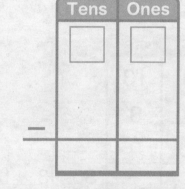

_____ pennies

5. **Higher Order Thinking** Fill in the missing numbers to make the subtraction problem true.

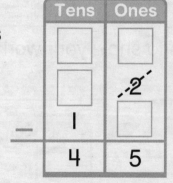

6. ✓**Assessment** To find 36 − 17, how can you regroup 36?

Ⓐ 2 tens and 6 ones

Ⓑ 2 tens and 16 ones

Ⓒ 3 tens and 16 ones

Ⓓ 4 tens and 16 ones

Name _____

Solve & Share

How is subtracting 23 from 71 like subtracting 3 from 71? How is it different from subtracting 3 from 71? Explain. Find both differences. Use blocks if you need to.

Tens	Ones
7	1
_	3

Tens	Ones
7	1
_ 2	3

_____

_____

_____

Find 43 − 18.
Show and write the subtraction.

Tens	Ones

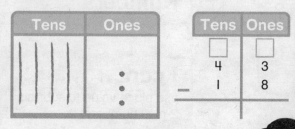

	Tens	Ones
	4	3
−	1	8

You can use a frame to write the subtraction.

There are not enough ones to subtract.
Regroup 1 ten as 10 ones.

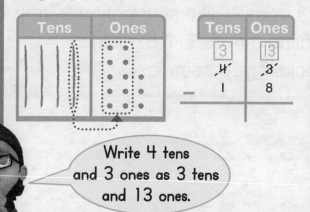

	Tens	Ones
	3 4	13 3
−	1	8

Write 4 tens and 3 ones as 3 tens and 13 ones.

Subtract: 13 ones − 8 ones = 5 ones
3 tens − 1 ten = 2 tens

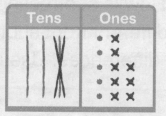

	Tens	Ones
	3 4	13 3
−	1	8
	2	5

So, 43 − 18 = 25.

Do You Understand?

Show Me! Why can you regroup 1 ten as 10 ones when there are not enough ones to subtract?

☆ **Guided Practice** ☆ Write each subtraction problem. Find the difference. Use drawings if you need to.

1. 34 − 15

	Tens	Ones
	2 3	14 4
−	1	5
	1	9

2. 52 − 31

	Tens	Ones
−		

3. 67 − 48

	Tens	Ones
−		

Sometimes you need to regroup. Sometimes you don't.

348 three hundred forty-eight

Independent Practice ☆ Write each subtraction problem. Find the difference.

4. 52 − 36

Tens	Ones

−
_____

5. 94 − 54

Tens	Ones

−
_____

6. 41 − 25

Tens	Ones

−
_____

7. 33 − 28

Tens	Ones

−
_____

8. 65 − 42

Tens	Ones

−
_____

9. 70 − 48

Tens	Ones

−
_____

10. 96 − 37

Tens	Ones

−
_____

11. 87 − 45

Tens	Ones

−
_____

Solve. Draw a model to help.

12. Higher Order Thinking Tia's basketball team
scored 61 points. They won by 23 points.   _____ points
How many points did the other team score?

13. **Model** Don has 72 marbles. Josie has 56 marbles. How many more marbles does Don have than Josie?

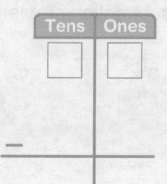

Tens	Ones

_____ more marbles

Can you use a drawing or objects to show the problem?

---

14. **Higher Order Thinking** Write a subtraction story using two two-digit numbers. Then solve the problem in your story.

_____

_____

_____

_____

_____

_____

Tens	Ones

15. ✅**Assessment** Eric can fit 90 cards in a scrapbook. He already has 46 cards in the scrapbook.

How many more cards will fit?

Ⓐ 44

Ⓑ 45

Ⓒ 46

Ⓓ 54

Name _____

Another Look! Remember the steps for subtracting.

Step 1	Step 2	Step 3
Think: Are there enough ones to subtract?	Regroup if you need to.	Subtract the ones. Subtract the tens.

HOME ACTIVITY Have your child use paper and pencil to solve 65 − 37. Have your child explain the steps he or she takes to subtract.

Write the problems in the frames. Find each difference.

38 − 13

Tens	Ones
3	8
− 1	3
2	5

54 − 17

Tens	Ones
4	14
5̶	4̶
− 1	7
3	7

Be sure to cross out if you regroup.

You can use drawings to help.

Write each problem in a frame. Find the difference.

1. 37 − 14

Tens	Ones
−	

2. 64 − 18

Tens	Ones
−	

3. 45 − 26

Tens	Ones
−	

4. 73 − 25

Tens	Ones
−	

Be Precise Decide which one item each child will buy. Subtract to find how much money is left.

Stickers   14¢
Craft sticks   36¢
Paint set   42¢
Crayons   58¢

---

5. Bonnie has 47¢.
She buys the

Tens	Ones

_____.

Bonnie has _____ ¢ left.   − _____

6. Ricky has 59¢.
He buys the

Tens	Ones

_____.

Ricky has _____ ¢ left.   − _____

---

7. Lani has 63 grapes. She gives 36 grapes to Carla. How many grapes does Lani have left?

_____ grapes

Tens	Ones

− _____

8. Write a number to make this a subtraction problem with regrouping. Then find the difference.

Tens	Ones

− 2	3

---

9. **Higher Order Thinking**
Use each number below.

1   2   4   5

Write the subtraction problem that has the greatest difference. Then solve.

Tens	Ones

− _____

10. ✔**Assessment** Norma has 48 buttons. Grace has 14 buttons. Connie has 29 buttons. How many fewer buttons does Connie have than Norma?

34   29   19   15
Ⓐ   Ⓑ   Ⓒ   Ⓓ

Name _____

Solve & Share

Find 52 − 24.
Use the bar diagram and subtraction frame
to help you show and solve the problem.
How can you use addition to check your answer?

I can ...
add to check my subtraction.

I can also reason
about math.

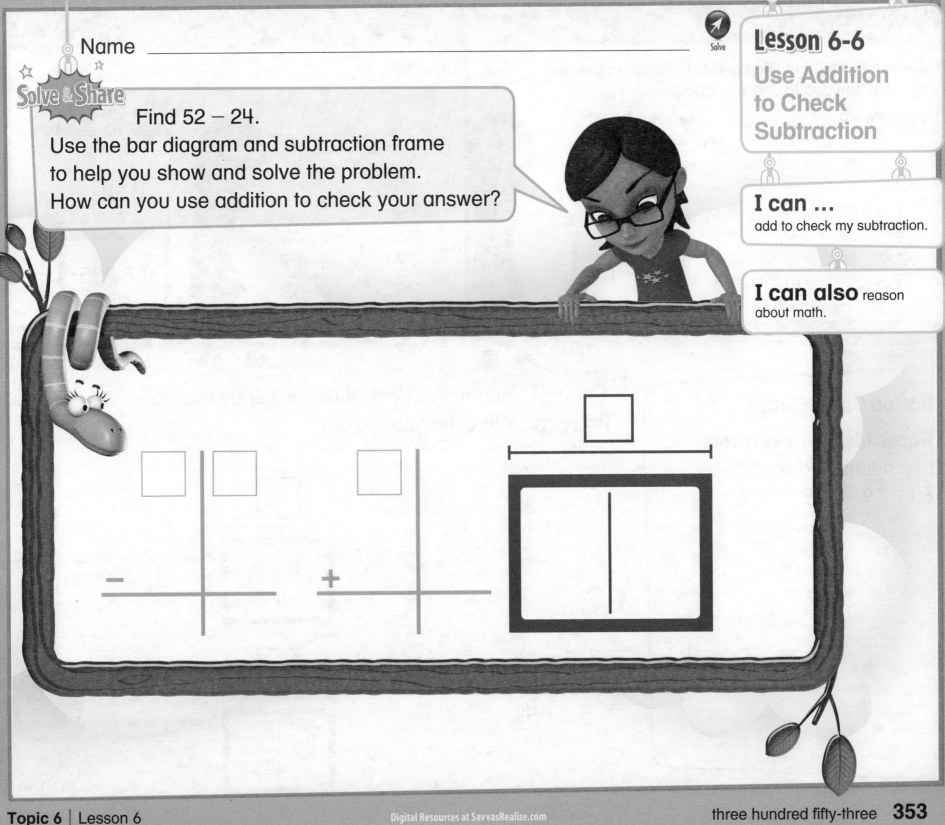

Remember that addition and subtraction are related.
So, you can add to check subtraction.

Find 24 – 9.

The sum of the parts equals the whole.

$$\begin{array}{r} 1\,14 \\ \cancel{24} \\ -\ 9 \\ \hline 15 \end{array} \qquad \begin{array}{r} 1 \\ 15 \\ +\ 9 \\ \hline 24 \end{array}$$

24

9	15

Find 52 – 17.

Add to check your subtraction.

The two parts equal the whole!

$$\begin{array}{r} 4\,12 \\ \cancel{52} \\ -\ 17 \\ \hline 35 \end{array} \qquad \begin{array}{r} 1 \\ 35 \\ +\ 17 \\ \hline 52 \end{array}$$

52

17	35

Do You Understand?

Show Me! Why can you use addition to check 63 – 19 = 44?

☆ **Guided Practice** ☆ Subtract. Check your answer by adding. Write the missing part.

1.

$$\begin{array}{r} 2\,12 \\ \cancel{32} \\ -\ 13 \\ \hline 19 \end{array} \qquad \begin{array}{r} 1 \\ 19 \\ +\ 13 \\ \hline 32 \end{array}$$

32

13	19

2.

$$\begin{array}{r} 78 \\ -\ 49 \\ \hline \end{array} \qquad \begin{array}{r} 29 \\ +\ 49 \\ \hline \end{array}$$

78

49	

You can show the parts in any order.

Tools   Assessment

Independent Practice

Subtract. Check your answer by adding.
Write the missing part.

3.

52
− 27

52

27

4.

80
− 14

80

14

5.

54
− 19

54

19

6.

75
− 62

75

62

7.

83
− 29

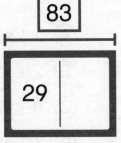

83

29

8.

48
− 21

48

21

9. Higher Order Thinking Maria uses 35 + 24 to
check her answer to a subtraction problem. Write two
subtraction problems Maria could have solved.

Problem Solving ☆ Subtract. Check your answer by adding.

10. Math and Science 62 students are doing science experiments. 48 students have cups of water. The rest have ice cubes. How many students have ice cubes?

$$\underline{} - \qquad \underline{} +$$

_____ students

11. Make Sense 37 students make clay pots. 16 students use brown clay. The rest use green clay. How many students use green clay?

$$\underline{} - \qquad \underline{} +$$

_____ students

12. Higher Order Thinking Write a subtraction story about 65 − 41. Solve the story. Check your answer by adding.

_____

_____

_____

13. ✓ **Assessment** Bill has 17 more craft sticks than Roger. Bill has 45 craft sticks. How many craft sticks does Roger have? Which shows the solution and how to check it?

Ⓐ 15 sticks; 30 + 15 = 45

Ⓑ 28 sticks; 28 + 17 = 45

Ⓒ 45 sticks; 28 + 17 = 45

Ⓓ 62 sticks; 45 + 17 = 62

Name _____

Another Look!

You can think of subtraction as starting with the whole.
Then you take away one part.
The other part is left.

$$\begin{array}{r} 37 \\ -\ 12 \\ \hline 25 \end{array}$$ Whole
Part
Part

$$\begin{array}{r} 25 \\ +\ 12 \\ \hline 37 \end{array}$$ Part
Part
Whole

Tens	Ones

Tens	Ones
and	and

HOME ACTIVITY Ask your child to find 65 − 32. Then have him or her use addition to show you how to check the subtraction.

To check your work, add to put the parts back together. Your answer should be the whole.

If no regrouping is needed, then add or subtract the tens and the ones.

Subtract. Check your answer by adding.

1.
$$\begin{array}{r} 86 \\ -\ 9 \\ \hline \end{array}$$ $$+$$

2.
$$\begin{array}{r} 54 \\ -\ 19 \\ \hline \end{array}$$ $$+$$

3.
$$\begin{array}{r} 63 \\ -\ 37 \\ \hline \end{array}$$ $$+$$

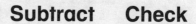

Model Subtract. Check your answers by adding.

4. Mei Ling has 71 marbles.
Then she loses 25 marbles.
How many marbles does Mei Ling have left?

Subtract   **Check**

_____ marbles

_ _____   + _____

Think about how addition and subtraction are related.

5. Denise has 51 beads.
Then she uses 32 beads to make a bracelet.
How many of her beads does Denise have left to use?

Subtract   **Check**

_____ beads

_ _____   + _____

6. **Number Sense** Write the number that makes each equation true.

$63 - 20 = 20 +$ _____

$58 - 40 = 18 +$ _____

$75 - 30 = 15 +$ _____

$89 - 46 = 30 +$ _____

In an equation, each side of the equals sign shows the same value.

7. ✓**Assessment** Lana subtracts to find $52 - 39$. Which addition equation could Lana use to check her answer?

Ⓐ $13 + 26 = 39$

Ⓑ $39 + 52 = 91$

Ⓒ $13 + 39 = 52$

Ⓓ $52 + 13 = 65$

Name _____

Solve & Share

Find 82 − 56. Use any strategy you have learned or your own strategy. Show your work. Explain why your strategy works.

I can ...
subtract 2-digit numbers and decide when to regroup and when not to regroup.

I can also reason about math.

Find 72 − 24.

One way is to break apart numbers.

72 − 24 = ?   72 − 20 = 52
      20   4   52 − 2 = 50
         2   2   50 − 2 = 48
                       So, 72 − 24 = 48.

Another way is to line up the numbers by place value.

$$\begin{array}{r} \overset{6\ 12}{\cancel{7}\,\cancel{2}} \\ -\ 2\ 4 \\ \hline 4\ 8 \end{array}$$

I get the same difference either way!

So, 72 − 24 = 48.

You can check your subtraction with addition.

My work checks. My subtraction is correct.

$$\begin{array}{r} \overset{1}{}\\ 2\ 4 \\ +\ 4\ 8 \\ \hline 7\ 2 \end{array}$$

Do You Understand?

Show Me! Could you solve 72 − 24 in another way? Explain.

★ **Guided Practice** ★ Use any strategy to subtract. Show your work. Check your work with addition.

1. 67 − 39 = _____

67 − 40 = 27

27 + 1 = 28

Check:

$$\begin{array}{r} \overset{1}{}\\ 2\ 8 \\ +\ 3\ 9 \\ \hline 6\ 7 \end{array}$$

2. 78 − 42 = _____

Name _____

Independent Practice

Use any strategy to subtract. Show your work.
Check your work with addition.

3. 73 − 34 = _____

4. 78 − 25 = _____

5. 83 − 46 = _____

6. 36 − 27 = _____

7. 98 − 51 = _____

8. 45 − 34 = _____

9. 86 − 29 = _____

10. 71 − 38 = _____

11. 85 − 23 = _____

Algebra Find the missing number.

Look for a pattern.
Use mental math.

12. 34 − 8 = 35 − ☐

13. 27 − 9 = 28 − ☐

Problem Solving

Make Sense Make a plan. Solve each problem. Show your work. Then check your work.

14. The hardware store has 32 hammers in stock. The store sells 16 hammers on Saturday. How many hammers are left?

_____ hammers

15. A barber does 15 haircuts on Monday. He does 28 haircuts on Friday. How many more haircuts does he do on Friday than on Monday?

_____ more haircuts

16. **(A-Z) Vocabulary** Complete each sentence. Use two of the words below.

addend   equation   difference   sum

$93 - 53 = 40$ is an _____ .

40 is called the _____ of 93 and 53.

17. **Higher Order Thinking**
Fill in the missing digits.

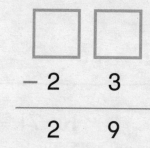

```
  □ □
- 2 3
-----
  2 9
```

18. **✓Assessment** Circle the problem that you will use regrouping to solve. Then find both differences. Show your work.

$56 - 38$ $74 - 52$

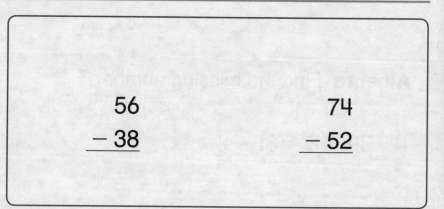

```
   56        74
 - 38      - 52
```

Name _____

Another Look! Find 82 − 37.

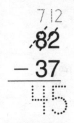

7 12
8̷2̷
− 37
45

Check

You can use addition to check your subtraction.

37
+ 45
82

Or you can break apart the numbers to check your work.

82 − 37 = ?

30   7

2   5

82 − 30 = 52
52 − 2 = 50
50 − 5 = 45

So, 82 − 37 = 45.

I can subtract in different ways. I will line up the numbers by place value!

There is more than one way to check your subtraction.

HOME ACTIVITY Write 78 − 29 on a sheet of paper. Have your child use pencil and paper to solve the problem. Then ask your child to explain how he or she found the difference.

Use any strategy to subtract. Show your work. Check your work.

I. 56 − 37 = _____

2. 46 − 18 = _____

3. 75 − 22 = _____

Topic 6 | Lesson 7

Digital Resources at SavvasRealize.com

three hundred sixty-three **363**

Make Sense Make a plan. Solve each problem. Show your work. Then check your work.

4. 45 basketballs are in a closet.
38 basketballs are full of air.
The rest need air.
How many basketballs need air?

_____ basketballs

5. Sue buys a box of 60 craft sticks.
She uses 37 craft sticks for her project.
How many craft sticks are left?

_____ craft sticks

6. **Higher Order Thinking** 36 berries are in a bowl. James eats 21 of the berries. Then he puts 14 more berries in the bowl. How many fewer berries are in the bowl now?

Is there a shortcut you can use?

_____ fewer berries

7. ✓**Assessment** Circle the problem that you will use regrouping to solve. Then find both differences. Show your work.

$83 - 45 =$ _____

$65 - 33 =$ _____

Name _____

Solve & Share

Trevor made 20 apple muffins for the bake sale. Ryan made 15 banana muffins. They sold 23 muffins in all. How many muffins are left?

Solve any way you choose. Then write two equations to show your work.

I can ...
use models and equations to solve word problems.

I can also model with math.

_____ ◯ _____ = _____

_____ ◯ _____ = _____

_____ muffins

Some students are in the gym. 13 students leave. Now there are 15 students in the gym.

How many students were in the gym at the start?

What is happening in the story?

You can write an equation. First, think about what you need to find.

How many students were in the gym at the start?

You can use a ? for the unknown.

$? - 13 = 15$

You can also use a bar diagram to show the parts and the whole.

?

13	15

You can add to solve the problem.

```
    1   3
+   1   5
---------
    2   8
```

So, 28 students were in the gym at the start.

Do You Understand?

Show Me! How does the bar diagram show what happens in the story problem?

☆ **Guided Practice**   Solve each problem. Show your work.

1. Some key chains are in a bag. Aki takes out 17 key chains. 14 key chains are left in the bag. How many key chains were in the bag at the start?

?

17	14

```
    7
+   4
-----
    3
```

_____ key chains

2. Some leaves are in a pile. 26 leaves blow away. 22 leaves are left. How many leaves were in the pile at the start?

?

26	22

_____ leaves

---

366 three hundred sixty-six

Topic 6 | Lesson 8

Name _____

Independent Practice Use a bar diagram to solve each problem. Show your work.

3. Some balls are in the closet. Mr. Thomas takes out 15 balls for class. Now there are 56 balls in the closet. How many balls were in the closet in the beginning?

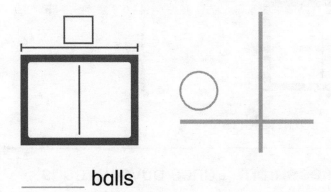

_____ balls

4. Corey buys a box of 96 paper clips from the store. He uses 34 paper clips. How many paper clips does Corey have left?

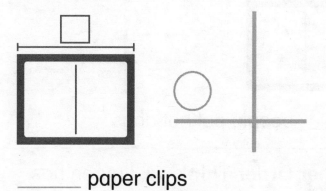

_____ paper clips

5. A.J. counts 44 acorns in his yard. He picks up 27 acorns. Then 16 more acorns fall from the tree. How many acorns are in the yard now? Show your work.

Step 1

_____ ◯ _____ = _____

Step 2

_____ ◯ _____ = _____

_____ acorns

Think about what to find first. Then use that answer to solve the problem.

Make Sense Make a plan. Solve each problem. Show your work. Then check your work.

6. 27 people are at a picnic. 14 people eat hamburgers. The rest eat hot dogs. How many people eat hot dogs?

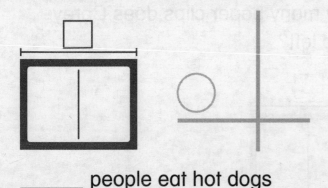

_____ people eat hot dogs

7. Some pumpkins are in a patch. 41 pumpkins are picked. Now there are 33 pumpkins in the patch. How many pumpkins were in the patch at the start?

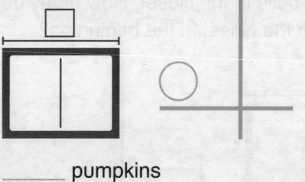

_____ pumpkins

8. **Higher Order Thinking** Lauren has a stamp collection. She gives Kristen 12 stamps and Ethan 15 stamps. Lauren has 22 stamps left. How many stamps did she have at the start?

Step 1

Step 2

_____ stamps

9. ✓**Assessment** Lance buys 48 eggs. He uses 24 of them for baking. Then he buys 12 more eggs. How many eggs does Lance have now?

Which set of equations can you use to solve this problem?

Ⓐ $48 + 24 = 72$
$72 - 12 = 60$

Ⓒ $48 + 24 = 72$
$72 + 12 = 84$

Ⓑ $48 - 24 = 24$
$24 + 12 = 36$

Ⓓ $48 - 24 = 24$
$24 - 12 = 12$

Name _____

Help   Tools   Games

Homework
& Practice 6-8
Solve One-Step
and Two-Step
Problems

Another Look! 52 cars are parked in the lot.
18 cars leave. Then 10 more cars leave.
How many cars are in the lot now?

Use the answer
from Step 1 to
solve Step 2.

Step 1: Subtract to find how
many cars are still in the lot
after 18 cars leave.

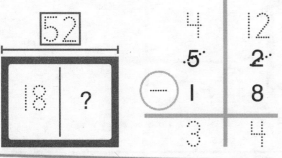

Step 2: Then subtract to find
how many cars are still in the
lot after 10 more cars leave.

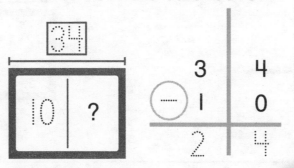

HOME ACTIVITY Have your
child solve this problem:
Some birds are sitting on
the roof. Then thunder
scares away 12 birds. Now
there are 32 birds sitting on
the roof. How many birds
were sitting on the roof at
the start?

Use the answer from Step 1 to solve Step 2.

1. 73 people are on the train. At a train stop 24 people get off
and 19 people get on. How many people are on the train now?

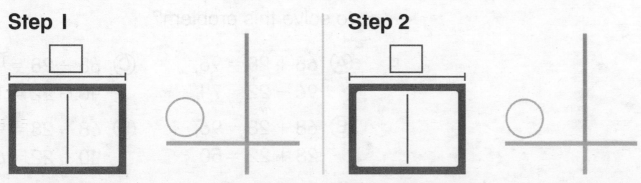

Step 1

Step 2

_____ people

2. Rosa's book has 88 pages in all. She reads some pages on Monday. She has 59 pages left to read. How many pages did she read on Monday?

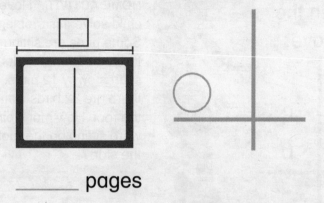

_____ pages

3. Jackie runs 19 laps on Monday. She runs 12 laps on Tuesday. How many laps did she run on both days?

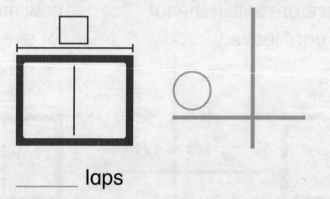

_____ laps

4. **Higher Order Thinking** Zak has a bag of cherries. He gives away 18 cherries to Tim and 18 cherries to Janet. Now he has 25 cherries. How many cherries did Zak have at the start?

Step 1

_____ ◯ _____ = _____

Step 2

_____ ◯ _____ = _____

_____ cherries

5. ✅**Assessment** There are 68 runners in a marathon. 28 runners finish the race. Then 22 more runners finish the race. How many runners have **NOT** finished the race?

Which pair of equations can you use to solve this problem?

Ⓐ $68 + 28 = 96$; $96 - 22 = 74$

Ⓒ $68 - 28 = 40$; $40 - 22 = 18$

Ⓑ $68 + 28 = 96$; $28 + 22 = 50$

Ⓓ $68 - 28 = 40$; $40 + 22 = 66$

Name _____

Solve & Share

Farmer Davis has 52 chickens.
He sells 15 chickens at the market.
How many chickens does Farmer Davis have now?

Use the bar diagram and equation to help you solve.
Be ready to explain how the numbers in the problem
are related.

I can ...
reason about word problems,
and use bar diagrams and
equations to solve them.

I can also add and
subtract two-digit numbers.

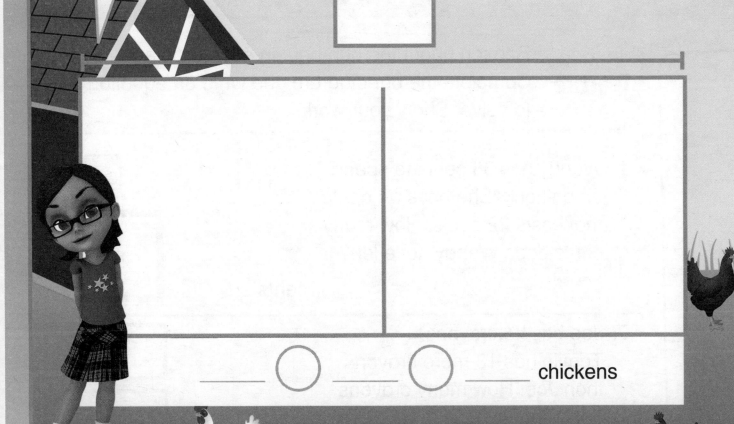

_____ ◯ _____ ◯ _____ chickens

Thinking Habits
How are the
numbers in the
problem related?

How can I show
a word problem
using pictures or
numbers?

45 beads are in a jar. Jenny uses some beads to make a necklace.
Now 17 beads are in the jar.

How many beads does Jenny use to make the necklace?

How can I use reasoning to solve the problem?

45 beads − beads in = 17 beads
necklace   left

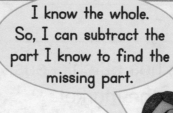

I can think about how the numbers are related. 45 − ? = 17 A bar diagram can show this.

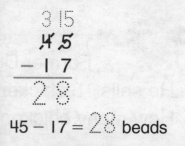

I know the whole. So, I can subtract the part I know to find the missing part.

45

? | 17

```
  315
  4̸ 5
− 1 7
─────
  2 8
```

45 − 17 = 28 beads

My bar diagram and equation show how the numbers relate.

Do You Understand?

Show Me! Why can you subtract 45 − 17 to solve 45 − ? = 17?

☆ **Guided Practice** ☆ Reason about the numbers in each problem. Complete the bar diagram and write an equation to solve. Show your work.

1. Wendy has 38 cents to spend on a snack. She buys an apple that costs 22 cents. How many cents does Wendy have left?

    — = _____ cents

   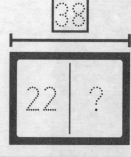

   38

   22 | ?

2. Joe has 46 crayons. Tamila has 18 more crayons than Joe. How many crayons does Tamila have?

   _____ ◯ _____ ◯ _____ crayons

Tools Assessment

Independent Practice Reason about how the numbers in each problem relate. Complete the bar diagram and write an equation to solve. Show your work.

3. **Math and Science** Andy's class wants to test samples of river water. They want to test 47 water samples. So far, they tested 34 samples. How many more samples do they need to test?

_____ ◯ _____ ◯ _____ more samples

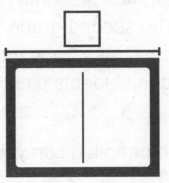

4. 93 dimes are in a box. Grant uses some to buy a game. Now, 66 dimes are in the box. How many dimes did Grant use to buy the game?

_____ ◯ _____ ◯ _____ dimes

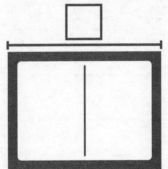

5. Maria paints 62 squares for a mural. Oscar paints 38 squares. How many more squares does Maria paint than Oscar?

_____ ◯ _____ ◯ _____ more squares

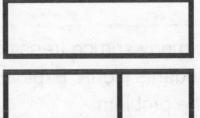

Problem Solving

Planting Trees

The second and third-grade students planted these trees in Wing Park. The second-grade students planted 26 of the spruce trees. How many spruce trees did the third-grade students plant?

38 Oak   **44 Spruce**

6. **Make Sense** What information can you get from the pictures?

_____

_____

_____

_____

7. **Model** Complete the bar diagram. Decide how the numbers in the problem relate. Then write an equation that shows how to solve the problem.

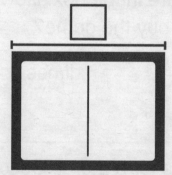

____ ◯ ____ ◯ ____

8. **Reasoning** How many spruce trees did the third-grade students plant? Explain how you solved the problem.

_____ spruce trees

Name _____

Another Look! Robin collects 36 acorns.
Trisha collects 19 more acorns than Robin.
How many acorns does Trisha collect?

HOME ACTIVITY Ask your child to find 76 − 42 by drawing a bar diagram and writing an equation. Then ask your child to explain what the numbers and symbols mean.

I can reason about the numbers. I will add 36 + 19 to find how many acorns Tricia collects.

This bar diagram shows comparison. The diagram and the equation show how the numbers and the unknown in the problem relate.

$$
\begin{array}{r}
36 \\
+ 19 \\
\hline
55
\end{array}
$$

36 ⊕ 19 ⊜ 55 acorns

Reason about how the numbers in the problem relate. Complete the bar diagram and write an equation to solve. Show your work.

1. The Tigers scored 53 points in a basketball game.
   The Lions scored 12 fewer points than the Tigers.
   How many points did the Lions score?

   _____ ◯ _____ ◯ _____ points

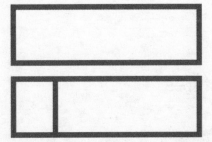

Vacation Pictures

Adam, Tessa, and Nicki take pictures on their vacation. How many fewer pictures did Adam take than Nicki?

Use the information in the table to solve.

Number of Pictures Taken

Adam	Tessa	Nicki
19	92	78

2. **Make Sense** Will you use each number in the table to solve the problem? Explain.

_____

_____

_____

3. **Model** Complete the bar diagram. Decide how the numbers in the problem relate. Then write an equation that shows how to solve the problem.

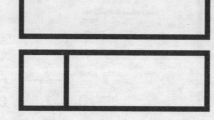

4. **Reasoning** How many fewer pictures did Adam take than Nicki? Explain how you solved the problem.

_____ fewer pictures

Name _____

Point & Tally

Find a partner. Get paper and a pencil. Each partner chooses a different color: light blue or dark blue.

Partner 1 and Partner 2 each point to a black number at the same time. Both partners add those numbers.

If the answer is on your color, you get a tally mark.
Work until one partner gets seven tally marks.

I can ...
add within 100.

Partner 1							Partner 2
49	34	76	74	61	63	89	**40**
60	58	80	93	78	95	100	**25**
36	85	74	69	50	98	65	**14**
55	45	87	60	84	89	49	**38**
20							**29**

Tally Marks for Partner 1	Tally Marks for Partner 2

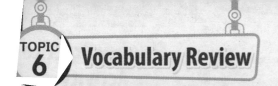

TOPIC 6 | Vocabulary Review

A-Z
Glossary

Word List
- bar diagram
- difference
- equation
- ones
- regroup
- tens

Understand Vocabulary

Write *always*, *sometimes*, or *never*.

1. A bar diagram shows subtraction. _____

2. An 8 in the ones place of a number equals 80. _____

3. A 5 in the tens place of a number equals 50. _____

Draw a line from each term to its example.

4. equation

5. regroup

6. difference

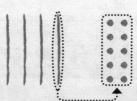

The answer to $75 - 23$

$72 + 25 = 97$

Use Vocabulary in Writing

7. Explain how you can make a model to show and help you solve the problem. Use terms from the Word List.

Molly has 64 marbles.
Leslie has 29 marbles.
How many fewer marbles does Leslie have?

_____

_____

_____

Name _____

Set A

You can **regroup** 1 ten as 10 ones when you subtract. Find 46 − 8.

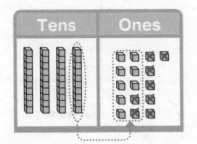

46 − 8 = _38_

Did you need to regroup?

(Yes)   No

Set B

You can draw place-value blocks to help you **regroup**. Find 72 − 6.

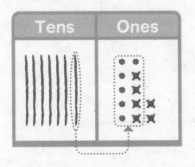

72 − 6 = _66_

Subtract. You can use place-value blocks to help. Regroup if you need to.

1. 61 − 3 = _____

Did you need to regroup?

Yes   No

2. 57 − 5 = _____

Did you need to regroup?

Yes   No

Subtract. Draw place-value blocks. Regroup if you need to.

3.

Tens	Ones
☐	☐
2	7
_	9

Tens	Ones

Find 53 − 6. Regroup if you need to.

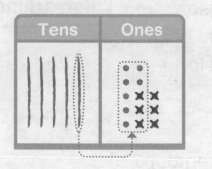

Tens	Ones
4̶	1̶3̶
5	3
−	6
4	7

Subtract. Use drawings if needed.

4.

Tens	Ones
3	8
−	9

5.

Tens	Ones
6	1
−	4

You can draw place-value blocks to help you regroup when subtracting two-digit numbers.

Find 43 − 15.

You can regroup 1 ten as 10 ones.

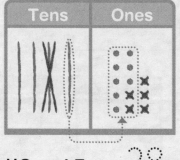

43 − 15 = 28

Tens	Ones
3̶	1̶3̶
4	3
− 1	5
2	8

Subtract. Draw place-value blocks. Regroup if you need to.

6.

Tens	Ones
7	2
− 3	6

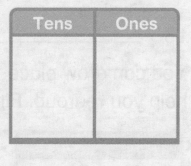

Tens	Ones

Name _____

Set E

You can write subtraction problems in a frame. Find 52 − 33. Draw pictures if needed.

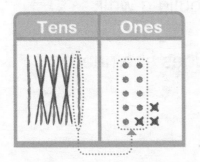

Tens	Ones
⁴4	¹12
.5.	.2.
− 3	3
1	9

Write each subtraction problem in the frame. Find the difference.

7. 84 − 47

Tens	Ones
□	□
−	

8. 62 − 36

Tens	Ones
□	□
−	

Set F

You can check subtraction by adding. The sum of the parts equals the whole.

```
  4 8        32
− 1 6      + 1 6
  32         4 8
```

48

| 16 | 32 |

Subtract. Check your answer by adding.

9.
```
  6 7
− 4 8
```

10.
```
  4 9
− 2 7
```

11.
```
  9 5
− 4 3
```

12.
```
  7 0
− 3 6
```

Thinking Habits

Reasoning

What do the numbers and symbols in the problem mean?

How are the numbers in the problem related?

How can I show a word problem using pictures or numbers?

Complete the bar diagram and write an equation to show the problem. Then solve. Show your work.

13. 94 bricks are needed to build a wall.
Lindy has 65 bricks.
How many more bricks does she need?

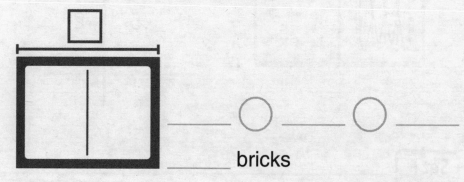

_____ bricks

14. Explain why making a bar diagram can help you solve the problem above.

_____

_____

_____

_____

Name _____

1. Would you regroup to find each difference? Choose Yes or No.

$45 - 8 = ?$ ○ Yes   ○ No

$51 - 9 = ?$ ○ Yes   ○ No

$77 - 6 = ?$ ○ Yes   ○ No

$83 - 4 = ?$ ○ Yes   ○ No

2. Sam has 74 books.
He puts 28 books on a shelf.
How many books are **NOT** on the shelf? Show your work.

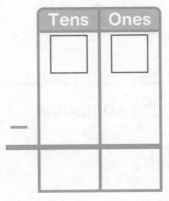

_____ books are **NOT** on the shelf.

3. Ryan has 46 marbles.
John has 4 fewer marbles than Ryan.
John gives 9 marbles to his friend.
How many marbles does John have now?

Ⓐ 23

Ⓑ 33

Ⓒ 35

Ⓓ 42

4. A ship has 68 round windows.
The ship also has 16 square windows.
7 of the windows are broken.
How many windows are **NOT** broken?

Ⓐ 45

Ⓑ 61

Ⓒ 77

Ⓓ 91

5. Choose all of the problems that you will solve by regrouping.

☐ 45 − 0 = ?

☐ 68 − 49 = ?

☐ 84 − 37 = ?

☐ 99 − 33 = ?

6. Ben wants to find 54 − 18.
How can he regroup 54?

Ⓐ 4 tens and 4 ones

Ⓑ 4 tens and 14 ones

Ⓒ 5 tens and 4 ones

Ⓓ 6 tens and 14 ones

7. Jason has 86 photos in his computer.
He deletes 61 photos.
How many photos are left?

Use the frame to help you.

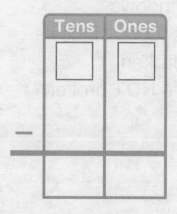

Ⓐ 5   Ⓑ 15   Ⓒ 25   Ⓓ 35

8. Claire has 53 beads.
Grace has 26 beads.
Bella has 39 beads.
How many fewer beads does
Bella have than Claire?

Show your work.

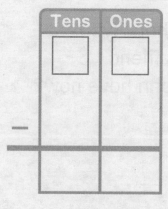

_____ fewer beads

9. Circle the problem that you will use regrouping to solve.
Then explain how you know.

$$54 - 23 \qquad 82 - 44$$

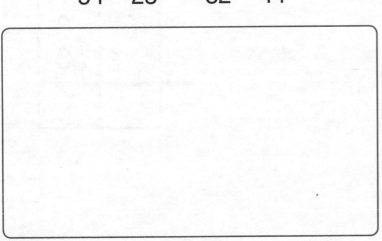

10. A book has 72 pages.
Dan reads 38 pages on Monday.
He reads 26 pages on Tuesday.
How many pages does Dan have left to read?

Which pair of equations can you use to solve the problem?

Ⓐ $38 + 26 = 64$
      $72 - 64 = 8$

Ⓒ $72 + 26 = 98$
      $98 - 38 = 60$

Ⓑ $72 - 38 = 34$
      $34 + 26 = 60$

Ⓓ $72 - 26 = 46$
      $46 + 38 = 84$

11. Part A
Subtract. Write the missing part in the bar diagram.

$$\begin{array}{r} 24 \\ -\ 16 \\ \hline \end{array}$$

Part B
Which addition equation can you use to check your answer?

Ⓐ $24 - 8 = 16$

Ⓑ $8 + 8 = 16$

Ⓒ $16 + 8 = 24$

Ⓓ $16 + 24 = 40$

12. Peter collects 54 stamps. He gives 29 stamps to Ruth. How many stamps does Peter have now? Show the problem in the bar diagram with a ? for the unknown number. Then write an equation to solve the problem.

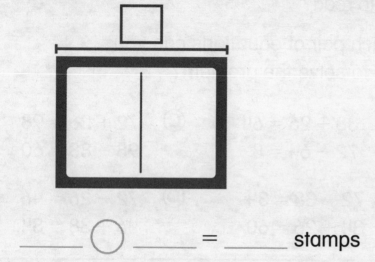

_____ ◯ _____ = _____ stamps

13. Match each number from the cards to a missing number in the problem. Write the missing numbers.

14. Find 72 − 38.
Use any strategy to solve. Then explain why your strategy works.

Name _____

Stamp Collection

Mary collects stamps.
The table shows the number of different kinds of stamps that she has.

Number of Stamps	
Flags	8
Butterflies	34
Birds	27
Flowers	61

2. How many fewer stamps with birds does Mary have than stamps with flowers?
Use subtraction to solve.
Then use addition to check your work.

_____ fewer stamps with birds

1. How many more stamps with butterflies does Mary have than stamps with flags? Show your work and draw pictures.

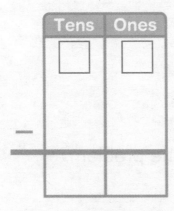

Tens	Ones
☐	☐

_____ more stamps with butterflies

3. Can you add in a different order to check your work in Item 2? Explain.

4. Luke also collects stamps.
He has 57 stamps.
His friend gives him 25 more stamps.

Then Luke gives away some stamps.
Now Luke has 44 stamps.
How many stamps did Luke give away?

Part A
How many stamps does Luke have
after his friend gives him more stamps?

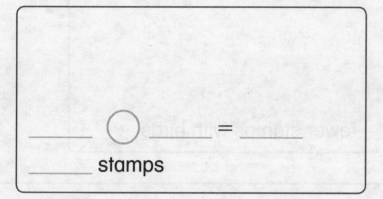

_____ ◯ _____ = _____

_____ stamps

Part B
How many stamps did Luke give away?

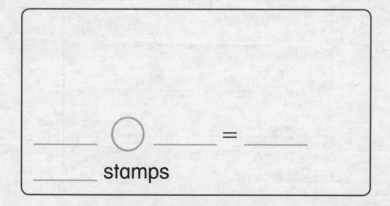

_____ ◯ _____ = _____

_____ stamps

5. Mary puts 54 of her stamps in a book.
The book holds 96 stamps.
How many more stamps can Mary put in
the book?

Part A
Complete the bar diagram to model the problem.

Explain how the bar diagram helps you
understand the problem.

_____

_____

_____

_____

Part B
Write an equation to solve the problem.

_____ ◯ _____ = _____

_____ more stamps

TOPIC 7
More Solving Problems Involving Addition and Subtraction

Digital Resources

Solve Learn Glossary

Tools Assessment Help Games

Essential Question: How can you solve word problems that use adding or subtracting?

This row of trees can help slow down the wind!

This is only one of the ways to help protect land from wind or water.

Wow! Let's do this project and learn more.

Math and Science Project: Solving Problems

Find Out Find and share books that tell about ways to protect land from damage that wind or water can cause. Compare the different ways to protect the land.

Journal: Make a Book Show what you learn in a book. In your book, also:

• Show ways to solve problems caused by wind or water.

• Show ways to solve problems using addition or subtraction.

Name _____

Review What You Know

1. Write the subtraction problem below as an **equation**.

$$75$$
$$- 30$$
$$\overline{45}$$

2. Complete the **bar diagram** to model $77 + 22 = ?$

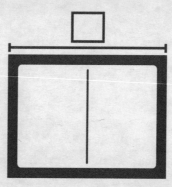

3. Circle the two addends below that are **compatible numbers**.

$$18 + 6 + 4 = ?$$

Adding to Check Subtraction

4. Use addition to check if the subtraction equation is correct.

$$51 - 22 = 29$$

Is it correct? _____

Subtracting to Check Addition

5. Use subtraction to check if the addition is correct.

$$37 + 26 = 53$$

Is it correct? _____

Number Story

6. Jim and Maria are counting birds. Jim counts 17 birds. Maria counts 33 birds. How many more birds does Maria count than Jim?

_____ more birds

Name _____

Solve & Share

Jenn has some red cubes and 11 blue cubes. She has 24 red and blue cubes in all.

She says the problem can be shown with the equation below.

$$? + 11 = 24$$

Draw what the ? represents.
Explain your answer.

I can ...
model problems using equations with unknowns in any position.

I can also use math tools correctly.

Robert has 27 toy robots. He buys some more. Now he has 58 robots. How many robots did Robert buy?

58 is the whole. 27 is one part.

You can show the problem with an equation.

$27 + ? = 58$

The ? shows the addend you don't know.

58

27	?

You can solve the problem by adding on from 27 until you get to 58.

$27 + 10 = 37$
$37 + 10 = 47$
$47 + 10 = 57$
$57 + 1 = 58$
$10 + 10 + 10 + 1 = 31$
So, $27 + 31 = 58$.

Robert bought 31 robots.

You can subtract to solve the problem.

$$\begin{array}{r} 58 \\ -\ 27 \\ \hline 31 \end{array}$$

You can check by adding.
$31 + 27 = 58$

Robert bought 31 robots.

Do You Understand?

Show Me! Could you show Robert's robot problem with the equation below? Explain.

$$58 = 27 + ?$$

☆ **Guided Practice** ☆ Write an equation with a ? for the unknown to model the problem. Then solve. Show your work.

1. Mary has some game tickets. She gives 14 tickets away and now has 17 tickets left. How many tickets did she have at first?

   Equation: $? - 14 = 17$ _____ tickets

2. Tamara has $25. She earns $34 more by working. How much money does she have now?

   Equation: _____ $ _____

Name _____

Independent Practice

Write an equation with a ? for the unknown to model the problem. Then solve. Show your work.

3. Erin has 32 books on her bookshelf. She gives some to friends and now has 19 books left. How many books did she give away?

Equation: _____

_____ books

4. A store sells 38 men's bikes and 47 women's bikes. How many bikes did the store sell in all?

Equation: _____

_____ bikes

5. **Math and Science** A field has 25 trees in it. 14 trees are new and the rest are old. How many trees are old? Write two different equations that represent the problem. Then solve.

Equation: _____

Equation: _____

_____ old trees

6. **Number Sense** Harry buys 22 fish. He has a round fish bowl and a rectangular fish tank. How could he place the fish in the bowl and tank?

Equation: _____

_____ fish in the bowl _____ fish in the tank

7. Model Rodney collects 17 leaves and Sheila collects 23 leaves. How many more leaves does Sheila collect than Rodney?

Equation: _____

_____ more leaves

8. Model Jun swims 18 laps and Mara swims 25 laps. How many fewer laps did Jun swim than Mara?

Equation: _____

_____ fewer laps

9. Higher Order Thinking Jim has 44 roses. 14 are white and the rest are red. How many are red? Write two different equations to model the problem. Then solve.

Equation: _____

Equation: _____

_____ red roses

10. ☑Assessment Some wolves howl in the woods. 12 wolves join them. Now 30 wolves howl. How many wolves howled at first?

Write an equation to model the problem. Use a ? for the unknown. Then solve.

394 three hundred ninety-four

Name _____

Another Look! Jamal has some green apples and 17 red apples. He has 29 apples in all. How many green apples does he have?

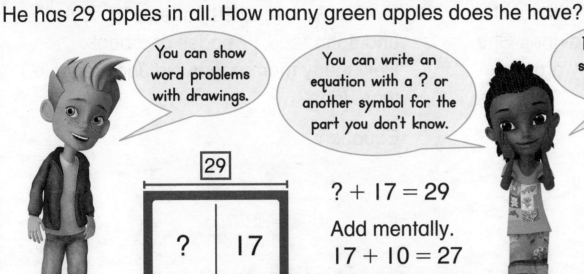

You can show word problems with drawings.

You can write an equation with a ? or another symbol for the part you don't know.

12 + 17 = 29, so Jamal has 12 green apples.

29	
?	17

$? + 17 = 29$

Add mentally.
$17 + 10 = 27$
$27 + 2 = 29$

HOME ACTIVITY Ask your child to write an equation for each of 2 different problems you make up. Then have him or her show you how to solve the problems.

 Write an equation with a ? for the unknown to model the problem. Then solve. Show your work.

1. Jill bikes 15 miles in the morning and 17 miles in the afternoon. How many miles does she bike in all?

Equation: _____

_____ miles

2. Maria makes 21 thank you cards. She mails 13 of the cards. How many cards does she have left?

Equation: _____

_____ cards

Write an equation with a ? for the unknown to model the problem. Then solve. Show your work.

3. **Model** Latisha eats 12 grapes with lunch and then eats some more with dinner. She eats 26 grapes in all. How many grapes does she eat with dinner?

Equation: _____

_____ grapes

4. **Model** Jack read 24 pages of a book and John read 19 pages of a book. How many more pages did Jack read than John?

Equation: _____

_____ more pages

5. **Higher Order Thinking** A train has 43 cars. 15 cars are red and the rest are blue. How many blue cars does the train have? Write two different equations that represent the problem. Then solve.

Equation: _____

Equation: _____

_____ blue cars

6. ✅**Assessment** 63 boys enter a marathon. 48 boys finish the race and some boys do not. How many boys do **NOT** finish the race?

Write an equation to model the problem. Use a ? for the unknown. Then solve.

Name _____

Solve

Lesson 7-2

**Mixed Practice:
Solve Addition
and Subtraction
Problems**

Solve & Share

Aiden has 27 fewer crayons this week than last week. Last week he had 56 crayons. How many crayons does Aiden have this week? Show your work.

I can ...
use drawings and equations to make sense of the words in problems.

I can also model with math.

_____ crayons

Sally has 28 fewer blocks than Nigel.
Sally has 26 blocks.
How many blocks does Nigel have?

Let's think about who has fewer blocks and who has more blocks.

A bar diagram can help you think about the problem.

Nigel's blocks

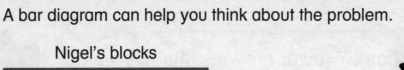

?

| 26 | 28 |

Sally's blocks   28 blocks fewer

26 + 28 = ?

Sally has 28 fewer blocks than Nigel. That means Nigel has more blocks than Sally. You need to add!

Nigel has 54 blocks.

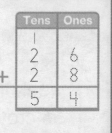

Tens	Ones
2	6
+ 2	8
5	4

Do You Understand?

Show Me! How are these statements alike and different? Cal has 12 fewer blocks than Mia. Mia has 12 more blocks than Cal.

Guided Practice Solve the problem any way you choose. Use drawings and equations to help.

1. Lakota has 11 fewer magnets than Jeffrey. Lakota has 25 magnets. How many magnets does Jeffrey have?

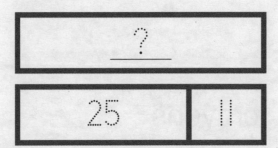

?

| 25 | 11 |

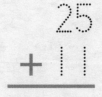

25
+ 11
_____

_____ magnets

398 three hundred ninety-eight

Topic 7 | Lesson 2

Independent Practice Solve each problem any way you choose. Use drawings and equations to help. Show your work.

2. There are 28 more students than adults at the school fair. There are 96 students at the school fair. How many adults are at the school fair?

_____ adults

3. Ellie the elephant has some peanuts. She eats 49 peanuts. Now Ellie the elephant has 31 peanuts. How many peanuts did she have before?

_____ peanuts

4. The blue team scores 16 fewer points than the green team. The blue team scores 41 points. How many points did the green team score?

_____ points

5. **Higher Order Thinking** Sean studies 16 fewer vocabulary words than Chris. Chris studies 10 fewer vocabulary words than Tia. Tia studies 34 words. How many words does Sean study? Explain your answer.

_____

_____

_____

6. Reasoning Kevin practices kicks for soccer. He kicks 13 times at recess. He kicks 14 times after school. Then he kicks 16 times before bed. How many practice kicks did Kevin take in all?

> I can think about what the numbers in the problem mean.

_____ kicks

---

7. Higher Order Thinking There are 48 red tacks and blue tacks in a bag. There are fewer red tacks than blue tacks. There are at least 26 blue tacks but no more than 30 blue tacks. How many of each color could be in the bag?

Complete the chart to solve the problem.

Red Tacks	Blue Tacks	Total
22	26	48
21		48
	28	48
19		48
	30	48

8. ✅Assessment Jim has 14 fewer baseball cards than Sara. Sara has 27 cards. How many baseball cards does Jim have?

Draw a line to show where each number and the unknown could be in the equation. Then solve.

| 27 | ? | 14 |

_____ − _____ = _____

_____ cards

Name _____

Help   Tools   Games

Homework
& Practice 7-2
Mixed Practice:
Solve Addition
and Subtraction
Problems

Another Look! A bar diagram can help you solve word problems.

Bridget has 15 fewer crackers than Jessica. Bridget has 20 crackers.
How many crackers does Jessica have?

Jessica's crackers

$$\begin{array}{r} 20 \\ + 15 \\ \hline 35 \end{array}$$

Bridget's crackers   15 crackers fewer

Jessica has __35__ crackers.

Bridget has 15 fewer, which means Jessica has 15 more. Add to find the number of crackers Jessica has.

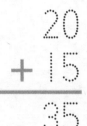

HOME ACTIVITY Tell your child Max has 10 fewer shells than Becca. Max has 20 shells. How many shells does Becca have? Then have your child write the equation. $20 + 10 = 30$.

Solve each problem any way you choose. Use drawings and equations to help. Show your work.

1. Ann puts 37 photos in one book and 24 photos in another book. How many photos does she use in all?

_____ photos

2. Jorge's puzzle has 20 fewer pieces than Rosi's puzzle. Jorge's puzzle has 80 pieces. How many pieces does Rosi's puzzle have?

_____ pieces

Solve each problem any way you choose. Use drawings and equations to help. Show your work.

3. **Reasoning** Lucy makes 37 get well cards and some thank you cards. She makes 60 cards in all. How many thank you cards does Lucy make?

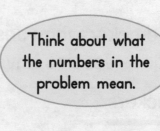

Think about what the numbers in the problem mean.

_____ thank you cards

4. **Higher Order Thinking** Jeff finds some bugs. He finds 10 fewer grasshoppers than crickets. He finds 5 fewer crickets than ladybugs. If Jeff finds 5 grasshoppers, how many ladybugs does Jeff find? How many crickets does he find? Write two equations to solve the problem.

_____ crickets   _____ ladybugs

5. ✓**Assessment** Sandy has 17 fewer hockey cards than Al. Al has 55 hockey cards. How many hockey cards does Sandy have?

Draw a line to show where each number and unknown could be in the equation. Then solve.

| 17 | ? | 55 |

_____ + _____ = _____

_____ cards

Name _____

Solve & Share

Erin has 17 more books than Isabella. Erin has 44 books. How many books does Isabella have?

Solve any way you choose. Show your work.

_____ books

Lesson 7-3

Continue Practice with Addition and Subtraction Problems

I can ...
use drawings and equations to make sense of the words in problems.

I can also model with math.

Julie has 18 more pictures than Landon.
Julie has 37 pictures. How many pictures does Landon have?

Julie's pictures

37

? | 18

Landon's   18 pictures
pictures   more

The diagram helps you show what you know.

Landon has 18 fewer pictures than Julie. You can subtract to find the answer.

$37 - 18 = ?$

2 17
3̸7̸
− 18
19

Add to check your answer.

19
+ 18
37

So, Landon has 19 pictures.

You can solve word problems using models, drawings, or mental math.

Do You Understand?

Show Me! Compare the two statements:
Sam has 18 more markers than Zoey.
Zoey has 18 fewer markers than Sam.

☆ Guided Practice ☆

Solve the problem any way you choose. Use drawings and equations to help.

I. The second grade has 19 more students than the first grade. The second grade has 68 students. How many students does the first grade have?

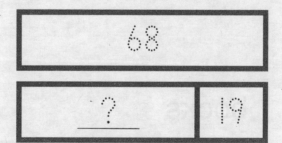

5 18
6̸8̸
− 19

_____ students

Name _____

Independent Practice Solve each problem any way you choose. Use drawings and equations to help. Show your work.

2. There are 11 more adults than children at a craft fair. There are 54 adults at the craft fair. How many children are at the craft fair?

_____ children

3. Caleb is 17 years old. His sister is 12 years younger. How old is Caleb's sister?

_____ years old

4. Dylan and his friends had some blueberries. They ate 39 blueberries. They have 21 blueberries left. How many blueberries did Dylan and his friends have at first?

_____ blueberries

5. **Math and Science** Addison made a dam with 18 more rocks than James. Addison's dam had 42 rocks. How many rocks did James's dam have? Explain your answer.

_____

_____

_____

_____

_____

Topic 7 | Lesson 3

four hundred five **405**

Solve each problem any way you choose. Use drawings and equations to help. Show your work.

6. **Reasoning** Connor has 39 sheets of green paper and some sheets of yellow paper. He has 78 sheets of paper in all. How many yellow sheets of paper does Connor have?

I can think about how the numbers in the problem are related.

_____ yellow sheets

---

7. **Higher Order Thinking** There are 58 red pens and blue pens in a bag. There are more red pens than blue pens. There are at least 36 red pens but no more than 40 red pens. How many of each color could be in the bag?

Complete the chart to solve the problem.

Red Pens	Blue Pens	Total
36	22	58
37		58
	20	58
39		58
	18	58

8. **✓Assessment** Andrew has 63 more beanbags than Evan. Andrew has 92 beanbags. How many beanbags does Evan have?

Explain how you will solve the problem. Then solve.

_____ bean bags

Name _____

Another Look!

Derek has some sheets of blue paper. He has 34 sheets of red paper. He has a total of 67 sheets of paper. How many sheets of blue paper does Derek have?

You know one of the parts and the whole.

$? + 34 = 67$

Subtract $67 - 34$ to find the missing part.

$67 - 30 = 37$ $37 - 4 = 33$

So, Derek has 33 sheets of blue paper.

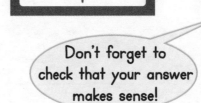

Don't forget to check that your answer makes sense!

HOME ACTIVITY Have your child solve the following problem: *Luke sold 27 more raffle tickets than Roger. Luke sold 53 tickets. How many tickets did Roger sell?* Ask your child to explain his or her solution.

Solve each problem any way you choose. Use drawings and equations to help. Show your work.

1. Joshua used 23 more craft sticks on his project than Candice. Joshua used 41 craft sticks. How many craft sticks did Candice use?

_____ craft sticks

2. Gavin painted 14 pictures last week. He painted some more pictures this week. He painted 25 pictures in all. How many pictures did Gavin paint this week?

_____ pictures

Solve any way you choose. Use drawings and equations to help. Show your work.

3. **Reasoning** Daniel tosses a number cube 19 fewer times than Jayden. Daniel tosses a number cube 38 times. How many times does Jayden toss a number cube?

I can represent a word problem with the correct numbers and symbols.

_____ times

4. **Higher Order Thinking** Wyatt has 34 blocks. Stella has 36 blocks. They give 14 blocks to Henry. Now how many blocks do Wyatt and Stella have together?

Complete the steps to solve the problem.

Step 1

Step 2

_____ ◯ _____ = _____

_____ blocks

5. ✅ **Assessment** Oliver runs 23 fewer laps than Nate. Nate runs 61 laps. How many laps does Oliver run?

Explain how you will solve the problem. Then solve.

_____ laps

Solve & Share

3 bees land on some flowers.
10 more bees join them. Then 4 bees fly away.
How many bees are left?

Solve the problem any way you choose.
Write equations to show how you solved each part
of the problem.

I can ...
model and solve two-step problems using equations.

I can also make sense of problems.

_____ ◯ _____ = _____   _____ ◯ _____ = _____

Bop picked 18 flowers and then 5 more.

He gave 10 flowers to Buzz. How many flowers does Bop have now?

Look for the hidden question that you need to answer first, before you can solve the problem.

I need to find how many flowers Bop picked in all, before I can solve the problem.

$18 + 5 = ?$

$\underline{18} + \underline{5} = \underline{23}$

Bop picked 23 flowers. Then he gave 10 flowers to Buzz.

$23 - 10 = ?$

$\underline{23} - \underline{10} = \underline{13}$

Now Bop has 13 flowers.

I added 2 ones to make the next ten and then added the 3 leftover ones to find $18 + 5 = 23$. Then I subtracted 10 from 23 to get 13.

Do You Understand?

Show Me! Tom bought 15 pencils and then 7 more. He gave 10 pencils to Nyla. If you want to find how many pencils Tom has left, why do you need to solve the first part of the problem before the second part?

☆ **Guided Practice** ☆

Solve any way you choose. Show your work. Write equations to solve both parts of the problem.

1. Carmen found 14 shells on Monday and 15 more shells on Tuesday. She found 6 more shells on Wednesday. How many shells did she have then?

$\underline{14} \oplus \underline{15} = \underline{29}$

$\underline{29} \oplus \underline{6} = \underline{}$

$$\begin{array}{r} \overset{1}{14} \\ + 15 \\ \hline 29 \end{array} \qquad \begin{array}{r} 29 \\ + 6 \\ \hline \end{array}$$

_____ shells

410 four hundred ten

Topic 7 | Lesson 4

Name _____

Independent Practice

Solve any way you choose. Show your work.
Write equations to solve both parts of the problem.

---

2. There are 6 red birds and 17 brown birds in a tree. If 8 more brown birds come, how birds will there be in all?

_____ birds

---

3. Erika saw 16 frogs on a lily pad and 8 frogs in the mud. If 7 of the frogs hop away, how many frogs will be left?

_____ frogs

Think: How can I break apart the problem into steps? What is the hidden problem that I need to solve first?

---

4. **Higher Order Thinking** Kevin has 15 photos in his scrapbook. He adds 21 photos. Then Kevin takes out some photos. Now he has 28 photos in the scrapbook. How many photos did Kevin take out?

_____ ◯ _____ = _____

_____ ◯ _____ = _____

_____ photos

Problem Solving ☆ Solve each problem.

5. **Model** There are 35 test questions. Kareem answers 10 of the questions. Then he answers 12 more questions. How many more questions does Kareem still need to answer?

_____ ◯ _____ = _____

_____ ◯ _____ = _____

_____ more questions

6. **(A-Z) Vocabulary** Circle the equations that have a **sum**. Underline the equations that have a **difference**.

$33 - 18 = 15$ $79 + 16 = 95$

$46 + 34 = 80$ $52 - 52 = 0$

7. **Algebra** Find the missing numbers.

$35 + \blacksquare = 100$ $\blacksquare = $ _____

$100 - \triangle = 18$ $\triangle = $ _____

8. **Higher Order Thinking** There are 25 friends at a party. Another 20 friends arrive. Then some friends leave the party. Only 7 friends stay. How many friends leave the party?

Write two equations to solve the problem.

_____

_____ friends leave the party.

9. **✓Assessment** Bill caught 22 fish and threw 6 fish back. He caught 8 more fish. How many fish does Bill have now?

Which equations can be used to solve the problem?

Ⓐ $22 + 6 = 28$ and $28 - 8 = 20$

Ⓑ $22 - 6 = 16$ and $8 - 6 = 2$

Ⓒ $22 - 6 = 16$ and $16 + 8 = 24$

Ⓓ $22 + 6 = 28$ and $28 + 8 = 36$

412 four hundred twelve

Topic 7 | Lesson 4

Name _____

Help   Tools   Games

Another Look! You can solve problems in different ways.

Jenna had 13 red markers and 15 blue markers. Then she lost 12 markers. How many markers does Jenna have left?

Step 1
Add to find out how many markers Jenna had in all.

Step 2
Subtract the number of markers Jenna lost.

$$
\begin{array}{r}
13 \\
+\ 15 \\
\hline
28
\end{array}
$$

$$
\begin{array}{r}
28 \\
-\ 12 \\
\hline
16
\end{array}
$$

> I broke apart the problem into two parts. I wrote the numbers like this. Then I used place value to solve each part.

13 (+) 15 = 28   28 (–) 12 = 16   16 markers

Solve any way you choose. Show your work. Write equations to solve both parts of the problem.

HOME ACTIVITY Make up story problems that take two questions, or steps, to solve. Ask your child to solve both parts of each problem.

1. There were 15 red apples and 6 green apples in a bowl. Eric ate 2 of the apples. How many apples are in the bowl now?

Step 1  _____ ◯ _____ = _____

Step 2  _____ ◯ _____ = _____

_____ apples

2. **Be Precise** Three students use the table to record how many jumping jacks they did each day. Complete the table and the sentences.

Hank did _____ jumping jacks on Friday.

Emma did _____ jumping jacks on Thursday.

Tana did _____ jumping jacks on Wednesday.

Jumping Jacks				
	Wednesday	Thursday	Friday	Total
Emma	30	_____	15	88
Hank	33	32	_____	85
Tana	_____	35	25	100

3. **Higher Order Thinking** Kendra drew 26 stars. She erased 12 stars. Then Kendra drew some more stars. Now there are 29 stars. How many more stars did Kendra draw? Write an equation for each part. Then solve.

4. ✅**Assessment** Ken needs to buy 100 nails. He buys 25 nails at one store and 36 nails at another store. How many more nails does Ken need to buy?

(A) 75

(B) 64

(C) 61

(D) 39

It helps to break apart the problem into steps.

Lesson 7-5

Continue to Solve Two-Step Problems

Solve & Share

You have 26 library books. You return some books. Then you take out 15 more books. Now you have 27 books. How many books did you return?

Solve any way you choose. Show your work.

I can ...
use different ways to solve two-step problems.

I can also make sense of problems.

Mia sees 15 yellow birds and 16 red birds. Some birds fly away and now Mia sees 14 birds. How many birds flew away?

I need to solve the first step of the problem in order to solve the second step.

Mia sees __31__ birds in all.

There are 14 birds left after __17__ fly away.

The bar diagrams helped me see the parts and the whole in each step of the problem.

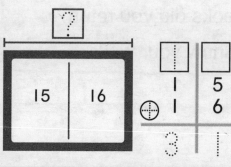

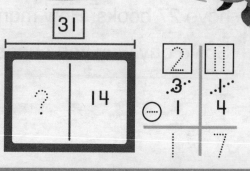

Do You Understand?

Show Me! Why do you need two steps to solve the problem above?

☆ **Guided Practice**   Complete the equations to solve.

1. There are some boys painting and 9 girls painting. In all, 17 children are painting. Then some more boys come to paint. Now there are 15 boys painting. How many more boys come to paint?

Step 1	**Step 2**
$8 + 9 = 17$	___ + ___ = ___
some boys girls children in all	some boys more boys boys in all

_____ more boys come to paint.

Name _____

Tools Assessment

Independent Practice Solve each problem any way you choose. Show your work.

2. Jake has 16 toy cars. Lidia has 5 fewer toy cars than Jake. How many toy cars do they have in all?

They have _____ cars in all.

3. Sandy has 12 balloons. Tom has 11 more balloons than Sandy. Some of Tom's balloons popped and now he has 14 balloons. How many balloons popped?

_____ balloons popped.

4. 25 wolves howl together in the woods. 14 wolves join them. Then 22 wolves run away. How many wolves are left?

_____ wolves are left.

5. **Higher Order Thinking** Explain how you solved Item 4.

_____

_____

_____

_____

6. **Make Sense** Tim bakes 24 more muffins than Gina. Gina bakes 13 muffins. Lea bakes 16 fewer muffins than Tim.

   How many muffins does Lea bake?

I can check that my work and answer make sense.

_____ muffins

7. **Higher Order Thinking** Write a two-step math story using the numbers 36, 65, and 16. Then solve the problem. Write equations to show each step.

_____ ◯ _____ = _____

_____ ◯ _____ = _____

8. ✓**Assessment** There are 44 marbles in a jar. Some are red and 23 are blue. Julie adds 13 red marbles to the jar. Now how many red marbles are in the jar?

   Which equations show a way to solve the problem?

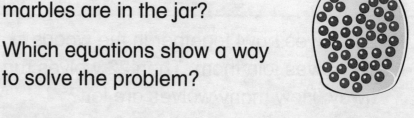

Ⓐ $44 - 23 = 21$
  $21 + 13 = 34$

Ⓑ $44 - 23 = 21$
  $21 - 13 = 8$

Ⓒ $23 + 21 = 44$
  $44 - 13 = 31$

Ⓓ $23 + 44 = 67$
  $67 + 13 = 80$

Name _____

Another Look! Use the answer from Step 1 to solve Step 2.

Tomas has 14 toy cars. Jonah has 6 more toy cars than Tomas. How many toy cars do they have in all?

Step 1: Add to find out how many toy cars Jonah has in all.

$$14 + 6 = 20$$

Step 2: Add to find the number of toy cars they have in all.

$$20 + 14 = 34$$

They have 34 toy cars in all.

HOME ACTIVITY Ask your child to solve two-step problems. Use small objects found at home as props.

Use the answer from Step 1 to solve Step 2.

1. Dani picked some red flowers and 9 pink flowers for a total of 21 flowers. Then Dani gave Will 5 red flowers. How many red flowers does Dani have left?

Step 1: Subtract to find how many red flowers Dani picked.

_____ – _____ = _____

Step 2: Subtract to find how many red flowers Dani has left.

_____ – _____ = _____

_____ red flowers

Mr. and Mrs. Morley picked their crops. Use the data in the chart to solve each problem.

Fruit and Vegetables Picked				
Apples	Peaches	Pumpkins	Corn	Squash
?	23	47	25	17

2. **Make Sense** Mr. Morley takes the apples and peaches to his fruit stand. He takes 58 pieces of fruit in all. He sells 13 apples. How many apples are at the fruit stand now?

_____ apples

3. **Higher Order Thinking** Write and solve a two-step problem about the data in the chart above.

_____

_____

_____

_____

4.  **Vocabulary** Complete the **bar diagram**. Use two possible **addends** with a **sum** of 25. Then complete the equation.

_____ + _____ = 25

5. ✓**Assessment** There are 21 students at the school picnic. Then 42 more students join them. Later, 30 students leave.

How many students are still at the picnic?

21   33   63   93
Ⓐ   Ⓑ   Ⓒ   Ⓓ

Name _____

Solve & Share

Write a number story for this equation.

$$20 = ? + ?$$

Then complete the equation to match your story.

I can ...
use reasoning to write and solve number stories.

I can also add and subtract two-digit numbers.

Thinking Habits

How are the numbers in the problem related?

How can I use a word problem to show what the equation means?

$$20 = \underline{} + \underline{}$$

Write a number story for 68 − 33. Then write an equation to match your story.

How can I show what numbers and symbols mean?

I think about what 68, 33 and the − sign mean in the problem. I can use that to write a story.

Subtraction stories can be about separating or about comparing. This story is about separating.

Harry finds 68 acorns. He gives 33 acorns to Joyce. How many acorns does Harry have left?

$$68 − 33 = ?$$

Subtract to answer the question in the problem.

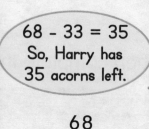

$68 - 33 = 35$
So, Harry has 35 acorns left.

$$\begin{array}{r} 68 \\ -33 \\ \hline 35 \end{array}$$

Do You Understand?

Show Me! Write a number story about comparing for $68 − 33 = ?$.

★ **Guided Practice** ★ Complete the number story. Then complete the equation to match the story. Draw a picture to help, if needed.

1. $47 − 18 = $ _____

   Blake collects __47__ cans.

   He recycles __18__ cans.

   How many cans does Blake have now?

   _____ cans

Tools Assessment

Independent Practice

Write a number story to show the problem.
Complete the equation to match your story.

2. $22 - 17 =$ _____

_____
_____
_____
_____

3. $84 - 62 =$ _____

_____
_____
_____
_____

4. $28 + 12 =$ _____

_____
_____
_____

5. $39 + 47 =$ _____

_____
_____
_____

Problem Solving

Toy Car Collection
The picture at the right shows a toy car collection. Use the picture to write and solve number story problems.

6. **Reasoning** Write an addition story about the toy car collection.

_____

_____

_____

7. **Reasoning** Write a subtraction comparison story about the collection.

_____

_____

_____

8. **Model** Write an equation for each number story that you wrote in Item 6 and Item 7. Then solve any way you choose. Show your work.

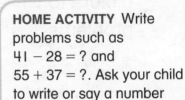

Another Look! You can write a number story about each problem. Then complete the equation to match the story.

22 − 15 = ?

There are __22__ red buttons.

There are __15__ blue buttons.
How many more red buttons are there than blue buttons?

22 − 15 = __7__

So, there are __7__ more red buttons.

36 − 17 = ?

__36__ grapes are on the table.

__17__ are red and the rest are green.
How many grapes are green?

36 − 17 = __19__

So, __19__ grapes are green.

HOME ACTIVITY Write problems such as 41 − 28 = ? and 55 + 37 = ?. Ask your child to write or say a number story about the problem. Have your child complete the equation to match the story.

Write a number story to show the problem. Complete the equation to match your story.

1. 31 − 8 = _____

_____

_____

_____

2. 23 + 37 = _____

_____

_____

_____

Bakery Muffins

The picture at the right shows information about muffins at Herb's Bakery. Use the picture to write and solve number story problems.

Herb's Bakery

33 Berry   18 Bran   29 Apple

3. **Reasoning** Write an addition story about the muffins at the bakery.

_____

_____

_____

_____

4. **Reasoning** Write a subtraction story about the muffins at the bakery.

_____

_____

_____

_____

5. **Model** Write an equation for each number story that you wrote in Item 3 and Item 4. Then solve any way you choose. Show your work.

Find a partner. Point to a clue. Read the clue.

Look below the clues to find a match. Write the clue letter in the box next to the match.

Find a match for every clue.

I can ...
add and subtract within 20.

Clues

A Is equal to 5 + 4 | **E** Is equal to 9 + 3 | **I** Is equal to 2 + 4

B Is equal to 8 + 7 | **F** Is equal to 13 − 9 | **J** Is equal to 5 + 6

C Is equal to 20 − 10 | **G** Is equal to 11 − 8 | **K** Is equal to 14 − 7

D Is equal to 12 − 7 | **H** Is equal to 7 + 6 | **L** Is equal to 10 + 6

☐ 10 − 7	☐ 19 − 9	☐ 8 + 8	☐ 12 − 8
☐ 18 − 9	☐ 13 − 8	☐ 13 − 7	☐ 8 + 3
☐ 4 + 9	☐ 15 − 8	☐ 9 + 6	☐ 6 + 6

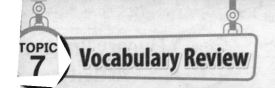

Glossary

Word List
- bar diagram
- compatible numbers
- difference
- equation
- open number line
- regroup
- sum

Understand Vocabulary

Write T for *true* or F for *false*.

1. _____ An equation is a model you can use to help solve a problem.

2. _____ 43 is the difference in the equation $43 - 16 = 27$.

3. _____ Addition and subtraction can be shown using a bar diagram.

4. _____ An equation is a model you can use to represent a problem.

5. _____ A sum is the answer to a subtraction problem.

Draw a line from each term to its example.

6. regroup

7. sum

8. open number line

The answer to $18 + 45$

15 ones = 1 ten and 5 ones

Use Vocabulary in Writing

9. Explain how you can count on to find $58 + 23$. Use at least one term from the Word List.

Name _____

Set A

You can model problems.

A store has some rings. Then 34 rings are sold. Now the store has 47 rings. How many rings did the store have at first?

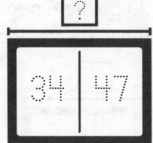

$? - 34 = 47$

```
  1
  47
+ 34
  81  rings
```

Write an equation with a ? for the unknown to represent the problem. Then solve using the bar diagram.

1. A store has 52 juice boxes. Then some juice boxes are sold. Now the store has 35 juice boxes. How many juice boxes were sold?

   Equation: _____

   _____ juice boxes

Set B

Trent has 29 more toy cars than Bill. Trent has 72 toy cars. How many toy cars does Bill have?

```
  6 12
  7 2
- 2 9
  4 3
```

This means Bill has 29 fewer toy cars than Trent. Subtract to solve. Bill has 43 toy cars.

Solve the problem any way you choose. Show your work.

2. A game has 19 more red cards than blue cards. The game has 43 red cards. How many blue cards does the game have?

   _____ blue cards

Lacie buys 28 peaches. She gives 12 to Ted. Then she buys 15 more. How many peaches does Lacie have now?

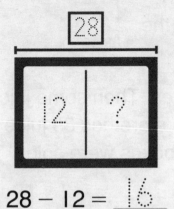 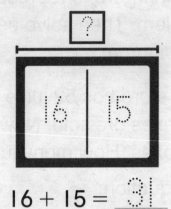

$28 - 12 = \underline{16}$　　$16 + 15 = \underline{31}$

$\underline{31}$ peaches

Use the answer from the first step to solve the second step. Use the bar diagrams to help.

3. Craig scores 27 points. Next he scores 33 points. Then he loses 14 points. How many points does Craig have now?

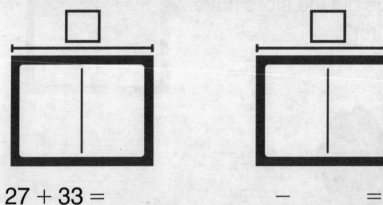

$27 + 33 = \underline{\quad}$　　$\underline{\quad} - \underline{\quad} = \underline{\quad}$

$\underline{\quad}$ points

Thinking Habits

Reasoning

How are the numbers in the problem related?

How can I use a word problem to show what the equation means?

Write a number story for the problem. Complete the equation to match your story.

4. $28 + 35 = \underline{\quad}$

_____

_____

_____

Name _____

1. Jodi has 28 apples. She buys some more.
Now Jodi has 43 apples.
How many apples did she buy?

Use the bar diagram to help you
write an equation. Then use
the open number line to solve.

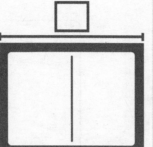

_____ ◯ _____ = _____

_____ apples

2. Alayna draws 18 more stars ✔ **Assessment**
than Pearl. Alayna draws
37 stars. How many stars
does Pearl draw?

Can you use the equation to solve the
problem? Choose Yes or No.

$37 - 18 = ?$ ◯ Yes ◯ No

$18 + 37 = ?$ ◯ Yes ◯ No

$18 + ? = 37$ ◯ Yes ◯ No

$? + 18 = 37$ ◯ Yes ◯ No

3. Emily has 17 fewer ribbons than Piper.
Piper has 48 ribbons.
How many ribbons does Emily have?

Solve any way you choose.
Show your work.

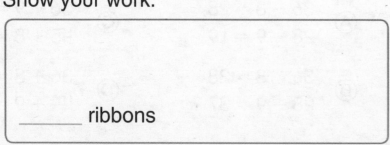

_____ ribbons

4. Write a number story for $72 - 36 = ?$.
Then solve the story problem.

$72 - 36 =$ _____

5. Joy needs 99 coats for children in need.
She gets 54 coats from her school.
She gets 22 coats from friends.
How many more coats does Joy need?

Write equations to solve.
Then write the answer.

_____ ◯ _____ = _____

_____ ◯ _____ = _____

Joy needs _____ more coats.

6. Shane has 27 more cards than Tom.
Shane has 62 cards.
How many cards does Tom have?

Explain how you will solve the problem.
Then solve.

Tom has _____ cards.

---

7. Grace found 36 shells.
She threw 8 shells back into the sea.
Then she found 9 more shells.
How many shells does Grace have now?

Which pair of equations shows a way to solve the problem?

Ⓐ $36 - 8 = 28$
    $28 - 9 = 19$

Ⓑ $36 - 8 = 28$
    $28 + 9 = 37$

Ⓒ $36 + 9 = 45$
    $45 + 8 = 53$

Ⓓ $36 + 8 = 44$
    $44 + 9 = 53$

Name _____

School Fair

Meadow School is having a school fair.
The table shows the number of tickets
Ms. Davis's class has sold.

Number of Tickets Sold	
Monday	42
Tuesday	17
Wednesday	21

1. How many fewer tickets did Ms. Davis's class sell on Wednesday than on Monday?
Complete the bar diagram to model the problem. Then solve.

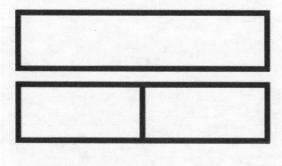

_____ fewer tickets

2. Ms. Davis says the class can have a party if they sell 95 tickets.

Part A

Write an equation to show how many tickets the class has sold.

Then solve the equation. Show your work.

_____ tickets sold

Part B

How many more tickets does the class have to sell to have a party? Explain.

_____ tickets

3. The table shows the number of tickets Mr. Rios's class has sold.

How many more tickets did his class sell on Monday and Tuesday than on Wednesday?

Number of Tickets Sold	
Monday	24
Tuesday	18
Wednesday	28

Write two equations to solve both parts of the problem.

_____ ◯ _____ = _____

_____ ◯ _____ = _____

_____ more tickets

Here are some models you can use or make.

Models
arrays
bar diagrams
drawings
equations
open number lines
place-value blocks

4. Part A
Write a number story about selling tickets for the school fair. Use numbers that you can add or subtract.

_____

_____

_____

Part B
Write an equation to match your story. Then solve any way you choose. Show your work.

Work with Time and Money

Essential Question: How can you solve problems about counting money or telling time to the nearest 5 minutes?

Digital Resources

Solve Learn Glossary

Tools Assessment Help Games

Different materials are used to make money!

How would you describe different types of money?

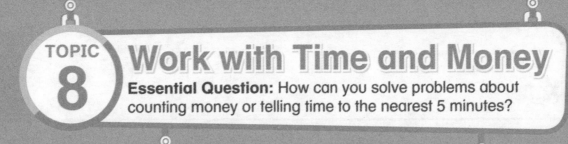

Wow! Let's do this project and learn more.

Math and Science Project: Money Matters

Find Out Collect examples of different types of coins and dollar bills. Describe how different coins and bills look and feel. Sort the money by size, color, and whether or not you can bend it.

Journal: Make a Book Show what you find out in a book. In your book, also:

• Tell how different types of coins are alike. Tell how they are different.

• Show as many different ways as you can to make 25¢.

Name _____

Review What You Know

A-Z Vocabulary

1. Draw the hands to show 8 **o'clock**.

2. Circle the number of minutes in one **hour**.

   30 minutes

   50 minutes

   60 minutes

3. Write the time below to the **half hour**.

   _____ o'clock

Doubles Facts

4. Write each sum.

$$7 \quad\quad 9 \quad\quad 10$$
$$\underline{+7} \quad \underline{+9} \quad \underline{+10}$$

Doubles facts are fun.

Array

5. Use mental math. How many squares are in the array?

   _____ squares

Math Story

6. Some pennies are in a cup. Jan takes out 22 of the pennies.
   Now, 14 pennies are left in the cup. How many pennies were in the cup at the start?

   _____ pennies

A-Z
Glossary

My Word Cards

Study the words on the front of the card.
Complete the activity on the back.

dime

nickel

penny

quarter

half-dollar

cents (¢)

I cent   10 cents
or I¢   or 10¢

My Word Cards

Use what you know to complete the sentences.
Extend learning by writing your own sentence using each word.

A _____
is 1 cent or 1¢.

A _____
is 5 cents or 5¢.

A _____
is 10 cents or 10¢.

The value of a coin is measured in
_____.

The symbol for cents is
_____.

A _____
is 50 cents or 50¢.

A _____
is 25 cents or 25¢.

My Word Cards

Study the words on the front of the card.
Complete the activity on the back.

A-Z
Glossary

greatest value

The quarter has the greatest value.

least value

The dime has the least value.

dollar

$1 or 100¢

dollar sign

$37

↑
dollar sign

dollar bills

tally mark

Ways to Show 30¢			
Quarter	Dime	Nickel	Total
I		I	30¢
	III		30¢
	II	II	30¢
I		IIII	30¢
		ⅢI I	30¢

My Word Cards

Use what you know to complete the sentences.
Extend learning by writing your own sentence using each word.

One _____

equals 100¢.

The coin that has the

_____

_____

is the coin that is worth the least.

The coin that has the

_____

_____

is the coin that is worth the most.

Use a _____

_____

to keep track of each piece of information in an organized list.

_____

can have different dollar values, such as $1, $5, $10, or $20.

A _____

_____

is a symbol used to show dollar money values.

My Word Cards

Study the words on the front of the card.
Complete the activity on the back.

A-Z
Glossary

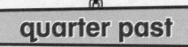
quarter past

4:15

It is quarter past 4.

half past

9:30

It is half past 9.

quarter to

3:45

It is quarter to 4.

a.m.

7:10 AM

breakfast time

p.m.

7:10 PM

dinner time

My Word Cards

Use what you know to complete the sentences.
Extend learning by writing your own sentence using each word.

A _____

_____

is 15 minutes before the hour.

---

30 minutes past the hour is

_____

_____.

A _____

_____

is 15 minutes after the hour.

Clock time from noon to midnight can be shown as

_____.

Clock time from midnight to noon can be shown as

_____.

Name _____

Solve & Share

Kelsey had 10 cents in her piggybank.
She finds 5 cents more and puts it in her bank.
Then Kelsey's mother gives her 20 cents to put in her bank.

How many cents does Kelsey have in her bank now?

I can ...
solve problems with coins.

I can also make sense of problems.

_____ cents

dime 10¢

nickel 5¢

penny 1¢

quarter 25¢

half-dollar
50¢

Micah has the coins shown below.
How many cents does Micah have?
Count on to find the total value.

Micah has 91 cents.
The cent sign is ¢.

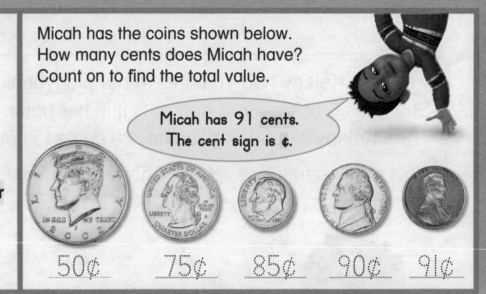

50¢   75¢   85¢   90¢   91¢

Do You Understand?

Show Me! How many quarters have the same value as a half-dollar?

How many dimes have the same value as a half-dollar?

How many cents would Micah have if he didn't have the half-dollar?

⭐ **Guided Practice**   Count on to find each total value.

1. Li has these coins. How many cents does Li have?

     ➡

25¢   50¢   _____ _____ _____   **Total**

---

2. Manny has these coins. How many cents does Manny have?

   ➡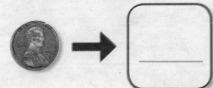

_____ _____ _____ _____   **Total**

       Topic 8 | Lesson 1

Tools   Assessment

Independent Practice   Count on to find each total value.

3. Jan has these coins. How many cents does Jan have?

            →

_____   _____   _____   _____

Total

4. Tim has these coins. How many cents does Tim have?

               →

_____   _____   _____   _____   _____

Total

5. Manny has these coins. How many cents does Manny have?

               →

_____   _____   _____   _____   _____

Total

6. Algebra Stacey had 92¢ this morning. She lost a coin.
Write the name of the coin Stacey lost.

            →

_____

92¢

Total

7. **Explain** Tori has 2 quarters, I dime, and I nickel. How many cents does Tori have? Show how you found your answer.

8. **Higher Order Thinking** Write a story about what coins you could use to buy an orange for 60¢.

9. ✅**Assessment** Lucas has these coins.

He is buying a gift for his brother. If he had one more nickel, which item would he have exactly enough money to buy?

Ⓐ   Ⓑ   Ⓒ   Ⓓ

10. ✅**Assessment** Jamie has 90¢. Which coins could she have? Choose all that apply.

☐

☐

☐

☐

Name _____

Help   Tools   Games

Homework & Practice 8-1
Solve Problems with Coins

Another Look! You can count on to find the total value of a group of coins.

Luanne has one quarter and two nickels. How many cents does Luanne have?

Start with 25¢. Count on by fives.

Think: 25¢   5¢ more   5¢ more

25¢   30¢   35¢

Tim has one half-dollar and two dimes. How many cents does Tim have?

Start with 50¢. Count on by tens.

Think: 50¢   10¢ more   10¢ more

50¢   60¢   70¢

HOME ACTIVITY Show your child 5 coins. Ask your child to find the total value and write that amount with a cent symbol.

Count on to find each total value.

1. Sarah has these coins. How many cents does Sarah have?

                  →

25¢   ____   ____   ____   ____

_____
Total

2. Marc has these coins. How many cents does Marc have?

                  →

____   ____   ____   ____   ____

_____
Total

Topic 8 | Lesson 1   Digital Resources at SavvasRealize.com   four hundred forty-seven   **447**

3. **Higher Order Thinking** Find the coins needed to buy each toy. Use the fewest coins possible. Write how many of each coin to use.

Count on as you use each coin.

4. ✓**Assessment** Will has 37¢. Which coins could he have? Choose all that apply.

☐ (quarter, dime, penny, penny)

☐ (quarter, penny, penny)

☐ (dime, dime, dime, penny, penny)

☐ (quarter, nickel, nickel, penny, penny)

5. ✓**Assessment** Jamal has these coins.

He needs 85¢ to buy a toy car.
How many more cents does Jamal need?
Draw the coin or coins he needs.

Topic 8 | Lesson 1

Solve & Share

Choose 5 coins. Which coin has the least value? Which coin has the greatest value? What is the total value of money you have?

I can ...
solve problems with coins.

I can also be precise in my work.

_____ greatest _____ ¢

_____ least _____ ¢

Total: _____ ¢

Seline has these coins.

How many cents does Seline have?

Start with the coin of **greatest value**.

Count on to the coin of **least value**.

So, Seline has 90¢.

50¢   75¢   85¢   90¢

Do You Understand?

Show Me! Why is it a good idea to put 1 nickel, 1 penny, and 1 quarter in a different order to find the total?

☆ **Guided Practice** ☆ Draw the coins from the greatest to the least value. Count on to find each total. You can use coins.

1.

⟨dotted circle⟩

60¢

25¢   50¢   55¢   60¢   **Total**

2.

⟨dotted circle⟩

_____

_____ _____ _____ _____   **Total**

Topic 8 | Lesson 2

Independent Practice   Count on to find each total value.

3. Eboo has these coins. How many cents does Eboo have?

The total is _____.

It helps to put the coins in order from greatest value to least value.

4. Hanna has these coins. How many cents does Hanna have?

_____ _____ _____ _____   The total is _____.

5. Mary has 3 dimes and 2 nickels. How many cents does she have?

_____

6. Danny has 4 nickels, 1 quarter, 2 dimes, and 3 pennies. How many cents does he have?

_____

7. **Number Sense** What 4 coins have a total value of 20¢? Draw the coins. Label the value of each coin.

8. **Math and Science** Greg's science class wants to sort these coins by their color. What is the total value of the silver coins?

_____ ¢

9. **Model** Draw the fewest number of coins to show 80¢.

10. **Higher Order Thinking** Write a story about finding 75¢. Draw the coins.

11. ✅**Assessment** Lydia has 3 coins. The total value is 40¢. She has 1 quarter and 1 nickel. Which shows her third coin?

40¢

Ⓐ   Ⓒ

Ⓑ   Ⓓ

Name _____

Help Tools Games

Another Look! To count coins, start with the coin that has the greatest value. Count on from the greatest to the least value.

Find the total value of the coins Seth has.
Draw an X on the coin with the greatest value.

HOME ACTIVITY Have your child take 4 coins from a cup of mixed coins and count on to find the value. Ask your child to record the value with a cent symbol.

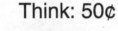 Think: 50¢   60¢   70¢   75¢

Start with 50¢.   50¢   60¢   70¢   75¢

 Find each total value. Draw an X on the coin with the greatest value.

1.

Start with _____.

_____ _____ _____ _____

2.

Start with _____.

_____ _____ _____ _____

Higher Order Thinking Solve each problem.

3. Megan had 50¢. She lost 1 nickel.
Circle the 5 coins that show how much she has left.

4. Yoshi had 55¢. He gave his sister a dime.
Circle the 3 coins that show how much he has left.

5. Kayla had 60¢. She gave her brother 4 pennies.
Circle the 3 coins that show how much she has left.

6. **A-Z** **Vocabulary** Circle the **nickel**. Put a square around the **half-dollar**. What is the total value of all the money?

_____ ¢

7. ✓**Assessment** Karen has 85¢. She has a half-dollar and a dime. Which other coin does Karen have?

(A)

(B)

(C)

(D)

Solve & Share

What is one way you can show 100¢ with coins? Use coins to model. Draw and label the coins you use.

I can ...
solve problems with dollar bills and coins that model 100 cents.

I can also model with math.

100¢

Digital Resources at SavvasRealize.com

This is I **dollar**.
The **dollar sign** is $.

$1 bill
$1 = 100¢

Here are some other **dollar bills**.

$5 bill

$10 bill

$20 bill

Maria had these dollar bills. What is the total value?

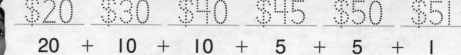

$20 $30 $40 $45 $50 $51

20 + 10 + 10 + 5 + 5 + 1

Count on from the greatest bill to the least bill. Maria has $51.

Do You Understand?

Show Me! How is counting dollar bills like counting coins? How is it different?

☆ **Guided Practice** Solve each problem.

I. Mr. Park has these dollar bills. Count on to find the total value.

_____

2. Ms. Lenz has these dollar bills. Count on to find the total value.

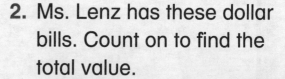

_____

Remember to count from the greatest bill to the least bill.

456 four hundred fifty-six

Topic 8 | Lesson 3

Independent Practice ☆ Solve each problem.

3. Mr. Higgins has these dollar bills.
Count on to find the total value.

_____

4. Ms. Nguen has these dollar bills.
Count on to find the total value.

_____

5. Mr. Abreu has these dollar bills.
Count on to find the total value.

_____

6. Ms. Wills has these dollar bills.
Count on to find the total value.

_____

7. Number Sense Mr. Anson has $26 in his wallet.
What is the least number of bills he can have?
Draw the bills.

_____ bills

Problem Solving ☆ Solve each problem.

8. **Model** Diana buys shoes on sale for $28. Draw dollar bills that she could use to pay for the shoes.

9. Mrs. Baker has two $10 bills and three $5 bills in her purse. Does she have enough money to buy a dress that costs $33? Explain.

10. **Higher Order Thinking** Roger buys a baseball bat that costs $27. He pays the clerk with two $20 bills. What bills can the clerk give him back as change?

11. ✅**Assessment** The dollar bills below show the total cost of tickets for a soccer game.

How much do the tickets cost?

$5	$31	$40	$41
Ⓐ	Ⓑ	Ⓒ	Ⓓ

Topic 8 | Lesson 3

Name _____

Help   Tools   Games

Another Look! What is the total value of the dollar bills shown below?

Count on from greatest bill to least bill to find the total value of dollar bills.

HOME ACTIVITY Have your child make different groups of dollar bills that total $37.

$20 $30 $40 $45 $46

20 + 10 + 10 + 5 + 1

Solve each problem.

1. Ms. Lopez has these dollar bills. Count on to find the total value.

2. Ms. Lenz has these dollar bills. Count on to find the total value.

3. Jack buys a bicycle on sale for $59. Draw dollar bills that he could use to pay for the bike.

4. **Look for Patterns** Marvin counts six $5 bills. Write each value that he counts. What pattern do you see in the ones digits of the values he counts?

_____

_____

_____

_____

5. **Higher Order Thinking** Maria has two $20 bills, three $5 bills, and four $1 bills. What other bill or bills does she need to buy a present that costs $69?

6. **Assessment** The dollar bills below show the money that Sam has saved.

How much money has Sam saved?

$52 $43 $42 $5

Ⓐ   Ⓑ   Ⓒ   Ⓓ

Name _____

Solve & Share

Timmy takes money out of his piggy bank.
He takes out two $10 bills, three $5 bills, and 6 $1 bills.
How much money does Timmy take out?

Draw a picture to show your work.

I can ...
solve problems with dollar bills.

I can also model with math.

$ _____

Chloe has a $20 bill and a $1 bill. Her sister Violet has $6 less than Chloe. Do they have enough money to buy a $35 scarf for their mother?

$35

You can show how much money Chloe has with a $20 bill and a $1 bill.

$20 + $1 = $21

 $20

 $1

You can find how much money Violet has by subtracting $21 − $6.

$21 − $6 = $15

 $10

 $5

Add to find if Chloe and Violet have enough money to buy the scarf.

$21 + $15 = $36

Violet could have a $10 bill and a $5 bill.

$36 is enough to buy a $35 scarf.

Do You Understand?

Show Me! How can you keep track of the amounts of money in the word problem?

Guided Practice

Solve each problem any way you choose. Show your work.

1. Sam had some money in his wallet. He went to the carnival and spent $12. Now Sam has $5. How much was in his wallet before the carnival?

$ _?_ − $ _12_ = $ _5_

$ _12_ + $ _5_ = $ _17_

$ _17_

2. Morgan has $7. Her grandmother gives her a $10 bill and a $5 bill. How much money does Morgan have now?

$ _____

Topic 8 | Lesson 4

Independent Practice ☆ Solve each problem any way you choose. Show your work.

3. Mia has two dollars. Ethan gives her two $5 bills. Noah gives her one $10 bill. How much money does Mia have in all?

$ _____

4. A sweater costs $38. Charlie has one $20 bill, one $10 bill, and two $1 bills. How much more money does he need to buy the sweater?

$ _____

5. Eli has $64 dollars. One of the bills is a $20 bill. What are the other bills Eli could have?

Draw a picture to show one solution.

6. **Higher Order Thinking** Jen bought three $5 raffle tickets and eight $1 raffle tickets. How much did Jen spend on raffle tickets?

Jen spent $ _____ on raffle tickets.

Explain how you solved the problem.

7. Make Sense Lily has two $10 bills, three $5 bills, and one $1 bill. She gives Grace $11. How much money does Lily have left?

8. Make Sense Isaac wants to buy a backpack for $20. He has two $5 bills and nine $1 bills. How much more money does he need to buy the backpack?

How much is two $10 bills?

$ _____

$ _____

9. Higher Order Thinking Henry has two $10 bills, two $5 bills, and three $1 bills. Mr. Harper has one $100 bill. Henry says he has more money because he has seven bills and Mr. Harper only has one bill. Is Henry correct? Explain.

10. ✅**Assessment** Olivia has one $20 bill, three $5 bills, and nine $1 bills. How much more money does Olivia need to buy a coat that costs $49? Explain.

_____

_____

_____

What bills can you use to show how much money Olivia needs?

_____

Name _____

Another Look! Kim has $4 in her bank.
She needs $20 to buy the gift she picked out for her mom.
How much more money does Kim need?

$20 − $4 = $ _16_

Kim needs $16 more.

Add to check your work.
$4 + $16 = $20
So, the answer makes sense.

HOME ACTIVITY Have your child use coins and bills to show various amounts in different ways.

$10 + $5 + $1 = $16

 Solve each problem any way you choose. Show your work.

1. Mrs. Brown had $16 dollars in her wallet. After shopping at the store, she now has $8. How much money did Mrs. Brown spend at the store?

$_____

2. Evelyn has $7. Liz gives her one $5 bill and two $1 bills. How much money does Evelyn have now?

$_____

Solve each problem. Show your work.

3. Be Precise Aiden has three $20 bills and two $10 bills. He wants to save a total of $95. How much more money does he need? What bills could they be?

_____

_____

4. Carter has one $20 bill, one $10 bill, four $5 bills and two $1 bills. Aubrey has two $10 bills, five $5 bills, and seven $1 bills. Who has more money? Explain.

_____

_____

_____

5. Higher Order Thinking Mark has $24. His brother has $8 more than Mark has. How much do they have in all?

Step 1

$_____ ◯ $_____ = $_____

Step 2

$_____ ◯ $_____ = $_____

Mark and his brother have $_____ in all.

6. ✅Assessment Emma has two $10 bills, three $5 bills, and two $1 bills. How much more money does she need to buy a game that costs $45? Explain.

_____

_____

_____

What bills can you use to show how much more money Emma needs?

_____

Name _____

Solve & Share

Suppose you want to buy a pencil that costs 35¢. How many different ways can you use nickels, dimes, or quarters to make 35¢? Show each way. Tell how you know.

I can ...
reason about values of coins and dollar bills, and find different ways to make the same total value.

I can also count or add coin values.

Quarter	Dime	Nickel	Total Amount
			35¢
			35¢
			35¢
			35¢
			35¢
			35¢

Thinking Habits

What do the numbers and symbols in the problem mean?

How do the values of the coins relate to the total?

I have some quarters, dimes, and nickels. I want to buy a banana.

30¢

How many ways can I make 30¢?

How can I reason about the different ways to make a total?

A table can show the coins. I can use **tally marks** to record the number of coins.

Ways to Show 30¢			
Quarter	Dime	Nickel	Total
I		I	30¢
	III		30¢

$$25¢ + 5¢ = 30¢$$
$$10¢ + 10¢ + 10¢ = 30¢$$

Tally marks make it easy to show the different ways.

Ways to Show 30¢			
Quarter	Dime	Nickel	Total
I		I	30¢
	III		30¢
II		II	30¢
I		IIII	30¢
		IIII I	30¢

I can write an equation to show and check each way.

I can make 30¢ in 5 different ways.

Do You Understand?

Show Me! Use the chart above. Write equations to show the ways to make 30¢ using dimes and nickels.

Guided Practice   Use reasoning. Complete the table.

1. Tony wants to buy a pencil.

55¢

He has half-dollars, quarters, and nickels. Find all the ways he can make 55¢.

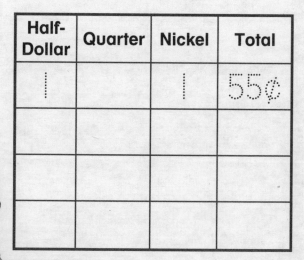

How do the tally marks relate to money values?

Half-Dollar	Quarter	Nickel	Total
I		I	55¢

Topic 8 | Lesson 5

Independent Practice ☆ Use reasoning. Complete each table.

2. Sue needs $12 to buy a book. She has $1 bills, $5 bills, and $10 bills. Find 3 more ways Sue can make $12.

$10 Bill	$5 Bill	$1 Bill	Total
I		II	$12

3. Raul wants to buy a bookmark for 14¢. He has dimes, nickels, and pennies. Find all of the ways he can make 14¢.

Dime	Nickel	Penny	Total
	II	IIII	14¢

You can write equations to check your work.

Number Sense What is the least number of bills or coins that you could use to make each amount? You can use the tables above to help.

4. $12

Number of bills: _____
Bills I would use:

_____

5. 14¢

Number of coins: _____
Coins I would use:

_____

6. Write an equation to show the total value of 2 nickels and 4 pennies.

_____

Problem Solving

Carnival Game Money

Don wants to use these coins to play as many carnival games as he can. Each game costs 40¢.

How can Don spend the coins that are shown at the right?

7. **Use Models** Choose from the coins shown. Show one way Don can spend 40¢ on one game. Write an equation.

_____

_____

8. **Make Sense** You used some of the coins for one of the ways. How will you know which coins are left to spend?

_____

_____

9. **Reasoning** Show how Dan can spend the coins to play games. Use tally marks in the table.

Which coin is left over?

Quarter	Dime	Nickel	Penny	Total

Topic 8 | Lesson 5

Help   Tools   Games

Another Look! Show three ways to make 25¢.
Two ways are shown in the table.

Use coins to help you find a
third way. Show I dime.
Make I tally mark.
How many nickels do you
need to add 15¢?

___3___

Make 3 tally marks.

Ways to Show 25¢

Quarter	Dime	Nickel	Total
I			25¢
	II	I	25¢
	I	III	25¢

HOME ACTIVITY Ask your child to use quarters, nickels, and dimes to show all the ways to make 70¢ with those coins.

Use reasoning to solve each problem.

I. Show three ways to make $20.
Use tally marks to record the bills.

Ways to Show $20

$20 Bill	$10 Bill	$5 Bill	Total

2. What is the least number of coins you
could use to make 45¢?
Make a table, if needed.

Number of coins: _____

Coins I would use: _____

_____

Least Number of Bills

The Williams family wants to buy these toys. They have $20 bills, $10 bills, $5 bills, and $1 bills. They want to use the least number of bills to pay for each item.

Which bills will they use to pay for each item?

3. **Explain** Marci thinks the family should use three $5 bills and three $1 bills to buy the doll. Does Marci's way use the least number of bills? Explain.

4. **Generalize** How can you find the least number of bills to use to pay for any of the 3 items?

5. **Reasoning** Complete the Williams's shopping card. Record the least number of bills they could use to pay for each item. Use tally marks.

Item	$20 Bill	$10 Bill	$5 Bill	$1 Bill
Doll				
Basketball				
Bicycle				

Name _____

Solve

Lesson 8-6
Tell Time to Five Minutes

⭐ ⭐

Solve & Share

An airplane is due to arrive at 3:15.
How can you show this time on the clock below? Explain.

I can ...
tell time to the nearest
5 minutes.

I can also look for
things that repeat.

Topic 8 | Lesson 6

Digital Resources at SavvasRealize.com

four hundred seventy-three **473**

Both clocks show 8:05.

minute hand

The minute hand moves from number to number in 5 minutes.

To tell time to five minutes, count by 5s. Both clocks show 8:35.

I can start at 8:00 and count by 5s to tell the time.

There are 60 minutes in 1 hour.

hour hand

The minutes start over again each hour.

Do You Understand?

Show Me! The time is 9:35. What time will it be in 5 minutes?

In 15 minutes?

In 25 minutes?

☆ Guided Practice ☆

Complete the clocks so both clocks show the same time.

1.

6:45

2.

3:25

3.

:

4.

5:40

Name _____

Independent ☆ Practice

Complete the clocks so both clocks show the same time.

5.

6.

7.

8.

9.

10.

11. Number Sense Complete the pattern.

12. Reasoning One of the clocks is running a little slow. The other clock is running a little fast. Estimate the correct time.

_____

13. Number Sense Look at the time on the first clock.
What time will it be in 5 minutes?
Write that time on the second clock.

_____

14. Higher Order Thinking Draw a clock that shows your favorite time of the day. Explain why it is your favorite time.

_____

_____

15. ✅ **Assessment** The minute hand is pointing to the 7. Which number will it be pointing to 10 minutes later?

Ⓐ 5

Ⓑ between 7 and 8

Ⓒ 8

Ⓓ 9

Name _____

 Help   Tools   Games

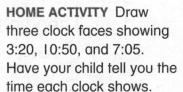

Another Look! You can use two kinds of clocks to tell time.

The minute hand moves from mark to mark in 1 minute.
There are 5 moves between each number. So, the minute hand moves from number to number in 5 minutes.

There are 30 minutes in a half hour and 60 minutes in an hour.
The hour hand moves from number to number every 60 minutes.

HOME ACTIVITY Draw three clock faces showing 3:20, 10:50, and 7:05. Have your child tell you the time each clock shows.

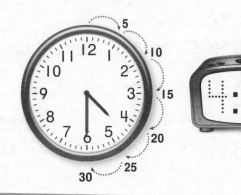

Count by 5s. Write the time.

1.

2.

3. **Generalize** The time is shown on the clock below.

6:05

Draw the time on the clock in the box at the right. Then complete each sentence.

The minute hand is pointing to the _____.

The hour hand is between _____ and _____.

Higher Order Thinking Each riddle is about a different clock. Solve the riddle and write the time.

4. My hour hand is between the 3 and the 4. My minute hand is pointing to the 7.

   What time do I show? _____

5. My hour hand is between the 5 and the 6. My minute hand is pointing to the 4.

   What time do I show? _____

6. My hour hand is between the 11 and the 12. My minute hand is pointing to the 3.

   What time do I show? _____

7. My hour hand is between the 1 and the 2. My minute hand is pointing to the 9.

   What time do I show? _____

8. ✔**Assessment** The clock shows the time that Sharon starts to walk to the library. The walk takes 10 minutes. At what time does Sharon get to the library?

   5:00   5:10   5:20   5:30
   Ⓐ   Ⓑ   Ⓒ   Ⓓ

Name _____

Both of these clocks show the same time.
How many different ways can you say this time?
Write each way.

I can …
say the time in different ways.

I can also be precise in my work.

Look at the times. Count by 5s to tell the time.
What are other ways to name the same times?

Times after the half hour are often read as times
before the next hour.

1:15

15 minutes
after 1,
quarter past 1

1:30

30 minutes
after 1,
half past 1

1:50

50 minutes
after 1

3:30

30 minutes
before 4

3:45

15 minutes
before 4,
quarter to 4

3:50

10 minutes
before 4

Do You Understand?

Show Me! Write two ways
to say 5:30.

☆ **Guided** ☆
Practice

Complete so both clocks show the same time.
Then circle another way to say the time.

1.

2:30

half past 2

30 minutes before 2

2.

6:45

quarter to 7

quarter past 6

Independent Practice

Complete so both clocks show the same time.
Then write the time before or after the hour.

3.

_____ minutes before 5

4.

quarter past _____

5.

25 minutes after _____

Higher Order Thinking Look at the clock to solve each problem.

6. What time will it be in 30 minutes?
Write this time in two different ways.

_____

7. What time will it be in 50 minutes?
Write this time in two different ways.

_____

8. **A-Z Vocabulary** Miguel is meeting a friend at **half past** 4.
Complete both clocks to show this time.

9. **Generalize** A train left the station at 6:55. What are two other ways to say this time?

_____

_____

10. **Higher Order Thinking** Draw a clock with hands that show 11:45.
Then write two ways to say the time.

_____

_____

11. ✔**Assessment** James gets home at 6:00. He starts his homework at quarter past 6. At what time does James start his homework?

Name _____

Another Look! Here are different ways to say time before and after the hour.

6:15

15 minutes after 6 or quarter past 6

6:30

30 minutes after 6 or half past 6

6:45

45 minutes after 6 or quarter to 7

2:40

20 minutes before 3 or 40 minutes after 2

HOME ACTIVITY Draw several clock faces. Have your child draw the time for 7:15, 2:30, and 5:45. Then have your child say the time using the terms *quarter past, half past,* and *quarter to.*

Count by 5s to tell the time. Write the time on the line below the clock. Then write the missing numbers.

1.

___30___ minutes after _____

or half past _____

_____

2.

_____ minutes after _____ or

_____ minutes before _____

_____

3. **Explain** The time is 6:10. Is the hour hand closer to 6 or 7? Explain your reasoning.

Higher Order Thinking Write the time. Then answer each question.

4. Nancy arrives at 10 minutes before 8.

School starts at

Is Nancy early or late for school?

_____

5. Sean arrives at quarter to 7.

Dinner starts at

Is Sean early or late for dinner?

_____

6. ✓**Assessment** Joyce wakes up at 10 minutes after 7. It takes her 40 minutes to get ready and walk to school. What time does Joyce get to school?

Ⓐ

Ⓑ

Ⓒ

Ⓓ

Name _____

Solve & Share

Look at the clock and tell what time Ethan wakes up for school. Write the time on the digital clock and circle morning or evening.

Lesson 8-8
A.M. and P.M.

I can ...
tell time and use reasoning to state if the event is happening in the a.m. or p.m.

I can also reason about math.

Ethan wakes up at:

Circle

morning

evening

You can use the terms **a.m.** and **p.m.** to tell about time.

Use a.m. for morning times. I wake up at 8 a.m.

Use p.m. for afternoon or evening times. I go to bed at 8 p.m.

I eat breakfast at:

(a.m.)　p.m.

I eat lunch at school at:

(a.m.)　p.m.

I eat dinner with my family at:

a.m.　(p.m.)

Do You Understand?

Show Me! What might you be doing at 6:15 a.m.? At 6:15 p.m.?

Guided Practice

Complete the clocks so both clocks show the same time. Then circle a.m. or p.m. to tell when you would do each activity.

1. Ride the bus to school

(a.m.)　p.m.

2. Do your homework

a.m.　p.m.

Name _____

Tools Assessment

Independent Practice

Complete the clocks so both clocks show the same time.
Circle a.m. or p.m. to tell when you would do each activity.

3. Take the bus home from school

a.m.   p.m.

4. Walk the dog before breakfast

a.m.   p.m.

5. Read a book before bedtime

a.m.   p.m.

6. Take swimming lessons on Saturday morning

a.m.   p.m.

7. Watch a movie on Friday night

a.m.   p.m.

8. Go to a party on Saturday afternoon

a.m.   p.m.

9. Higher Order Thinking Jen and Maria have dance lessons at the time shown on the clock.
Write the time two different ways. Is it a.m. or p.m.? Explain.

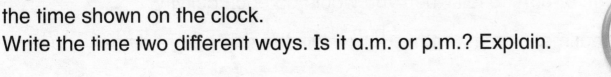

_____

10. Be Precise Draw hands on the clock to show what time your school begins each day. Then write the time. Include a.m. or p.m.

11. Math and Science Stargazing is looking at the stars. The best time to stargaze is on a clear moonless night.

Gina went outside to stargaze at 9:00. Is this 9:00 a.m. or 9:00 p.m.? Explain.

_____

_____

12. Higher Order Thinking Grace starts her homework at 4:15.
She finishes her homework 45 minutes later. Draw the hands on the clocks to show both times. Write both times on the digital clocks.

Circle a.m. or p.m. below to tell when Grace does her homework.

a.m.   p.m.

13. ✅Assessment Circle a.m. or p.m. to tell when you would do each activity.

Brush your teeth before bedtime   a.m.   p.m.   Walk the dog before dinner   a.m.   p.m.

Go to soccer practice after school   a.m.   p.m.   Watch the sunrise   a.m.   p.m.

Name _____

Help Tools Games

Another Look! Circle a.m. or p.m. to tell when each activity takes place.

Mom goes swimming in the morning.

I go to soccer practice after school.

Dad goes for a walk after dinner in the evening.

HOME ACTIVITY Write three things that you do at different times of the day. Have your child tell you whether you do these things in the a.m. or the p.m.

9:15

4:00

6:45

a.m. means before noon. p.m. means after noon.

(a.m.) p.m.

a.m. (p.m.)

a.m. (p.m.)

Complete the clocks so both clocks show the same time.
Circle a.m. or p.m. to tell when each activity takes place.

1. Eat a snack in the morning

10:15

(a.m.) p.m.

2. Brush your teeth after lunch

:

a.m. p.m.

Solve each problem.

3. **🔤 Vocabulary** Write an example of an event that could happen in the **a.m.** Write an example of an event that could happen in the **p.m.**

_____

_____

_____

4. **Higher Order Thinking** Guess what time it is. Right now, it is p.m.

In 10 minutes it will be a.m. What time is it now? Explain.

_____

_____

Write the time in the clock.

5. **✓ Assessment** Alexis wakes up in the morning at the time shown on the clock. What time does Alexis wake up?

Ⓐ 7:15 a.m.

Ⓑ 8:15 a.m.

Ⓒ 7:15 p.m.

Ⓓ 8:15 p.m.

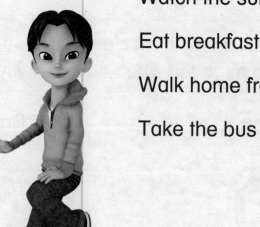

6. **✓ Assessment** Circle a.m. or p.m. to tell when you would do each activity.

Watch the sunset   a.m.   p.m.

Eat breakfast   a.m.   p.m.

Walk home from school   a.m.   p.m.

Take the bus to school   a.m.   p.m.

Name _____

Find a Match

Find a partner. Point to a clue. Read the clue.

Look below the clues to find a match. Write the clue letter in the box next to the match.

Find a match for every clue.

I can ...
add and subtract within 20.

Clues

A Is equal to $12 - 5$	**E** Is equal to $3 + 3$	**I** Is equal to $17 - 8$
B Is equal to $9 + 2$	**F** Is equal to $15 - 7$	**J** Is equal to $6 + 9$
C Is equal to $12 - 10$	**G** Is equal to $8 + 6$	**K** Is equal to $8 - 5$
D Is equal to $8 + 9$	**H** Is equal to $12 - 8$	**L** Is equal to $9 + 9$

☐ $8 - 0$	☐ $10 + 8$	☐ $10 + 5$	☐ $9 + 8$
☐ $10 - 6$	☐ $4 + 7$	☐ $7 - 4$	☐ $3 + 4$
☐ $8 - 6$	☐ $9 + 5$	☐ $14 - 8$	☐ $12 - 3$

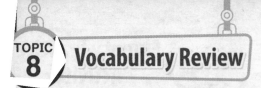

Glossary

Word List

- a.m.
- cents (¢)
- dime
- dollar
- dollar bills
- dollar sign
- greatest value
- half-dollar
- half past
- least value
- nickel
- penny
- p.m.
- quarter
- quarter past
- quarter to
- tally mark

Understand Vocabulary

1. Circle the name of the coin with the *greatest value*.

quarter   nickel   dime

2. Circle the name of the coin with the *least value*.

half-dollar   penny   quarter

3. Cross out the time that is **NOT** quarter past 5 or quarter to 5.

4:45   5:15   5:25

4. Cross out the time that is **NOT** half past 8 or quarter past 8.

8:30   8:45   8:15

When does each event happen? Write a possible time.
Use a.m. or p.m.

5. school ends

_____

6. eat breakfast

_____

7. sunrise

_____

Use Vocabulary in Writing

8. Explain how you can show ways to make 1 dollar (100¢) using coins. Use terms from the Word List. Give examples.

Name _____

Set A _____

When you count coins, start with the coin of greatest value.

Randi has the coins shown below. Count on to find the total value.

quarter (25¢) dime (10¢) nickel (5¢)

$\underline{25¢}$ $\underline{35¢}$ $\underline{40¢}$

Randi has $\underline{40¢}$.

Another Example

Duane has the coins below. How much money does Duane have?

$\underline{25¢}$ $\underline{50¢}$ $\underline{60¢}$ $\underline{70¢}$

Duane has $\underline{70¢}$.

Solve each problem.
Count on to find the total value.

1. These coins are in a jar. How many cents are in the jar?

Draw the coins in order.

Count on. _____ _____ _____

There is _____ in the jar.

2. The coins shown below are in a box. How much money is in the box?

There is _____ in the box.

Dollar bills are paper money and can have different dollar values.

$1 bill
$1 = 100¢

$5 bill

$10 bill

$20 bill

Matt has $56. Two of his bills are $20 bills. What other bills could Matt have? You can count on to get to $56.

$20, $40, $50 , $55 , $56
                +$10   +$5   +$1

The other bills Matt could have are a $10 bill, a $5 bill, and a $1 bill.

Solve each problem.

3. Mr. Park has these dollar bills. Count on to find the total value.

Remember to count from the greatest bill to the least bill.

_____

4. A cookbook costs $36. Mrs. Beeson has a $10 bill and a $5 bill. How much more money does Mrs. Beeson need to buy the cookbook?

$_____

Name _____

Set C _____

Thinking Habits

Reasoning

What do the numbers and symbols in the problem mean?

How do the values of the coins relate to the total?

Use reasoning. Finish the table.

5. Mitch has dimes, nickels, and pennies. Find ways he can make 11¢. Show a tally mark for each coin you use.

Dime	Nickel	Penny	Total
I		I	11¢

Did you find all the different ways?

Set D _____

It takes 5 minutes for the minute hand to move from one number to the next. Count on by 5s.

8:20

Read the time.
Write the same time on the digital clock.

6.

:

You can say the number of minutes before the hour or after the hour.

10 minutes before 5

(10 minutes after 5)

(10 minutes before 5)

10 minutes after 5

Circle the time each clock shows.

7.

5 minutes before 3

5 minutes after 3

8.

15 minutes before 10

15 minutes after 10

Use a.m. from midnight to noon.
Use p.m. from noon to midnight.

Walking the dog before bed

a.m. (p.m.)

Eating a morning snack

(a.m.) p.m.

Circle a.m. or p.m. to tell when you would do each activity.

9. Afternoon recess

a.m.   p.m.

10. Feeding fish after breakfast

a.m.   p.m.

Name _____

1. Chen has these coins.
How much money does Chen have?

Count on to find the total.

_____ cents

2. Ellen has 4 coins.
The total value is 46¢.
She has 1 quarter, 1 dime,
and 1 penny.
Which shows her fourth coin?

Ⓐ   Ⓑ   Ⓒ   Ⓓ

3. Nancy has 31¢.
Which coins could she have?
Choose all that apply.

☐

☐

☐

☐

4. George has quarters, dimes, and nickels.
Show all the ways he can make 25¢. Use
tally marks.

Circle the way that uses the least number
of coins.

Ways to Show 25¢			
Quarter	Dime	Nickel	Total

5. Mr. Zink has the dollar bills shown below.

How many dollars does Mr. Zink have?

$36 $31 $26 $5

Ⓐ   Ⓑ   Ⓒ   Ⓓ

6. Claire has two $20 bills, two $5 bills, and three $1 bills. How much more money does Claire need to buy a bike that costs $89? Explain.

What bills can you use to show how much money Claire needs?

7. Kay has saved $30.
Show three different ways to make $30. Use tally marks in the table at the right.

Circle the way that uses the least number of bills.

Ways to Show $30			
$20 Bill	$10 Bill	$5 Bill	Total

Name _____

8. Sandy wakes up in the morning at the time shown on the clock.

What time does Sandy wake up?

Ⓐ 5:10 a.m

Ⓒ 5:10 p.m.

Ⓑ 6:10 a.m.

Ⓓ 6:10 p.m.

9. Sara's baseball game starts at the time shown on the clock.

Is this the time her game starts?
Choose Yes or No.

45 minutes after 4	○ Yes	○ No
15 minutes before 5	○ Yes	○ No
quarter to 4	○ Yes	○ No
quarter to 5	○ Yes	○ No

10. The clock shows the time that Holly leaves for school.
It takes 15 minutes to walk to school.
At what time will Holly arrive at school?
Choose all that apply.

☐ half past 7

☐ quarter past 8

☐ 30 minutes after 8

☐ half past 8

11. The first clock shows the time the sun rises.
Write the same time on the second clock.
Then circle a.m. or p.m.

a.m.   p.m.

12. Look at the time on the first clock. What time will it be in 10 minutes? Write that time on the second clock.

13. Circle a.m. or p.m. to tell when you would do each activity.

Watch the sunset at 7:40.   a.m.   p.m.

Take a music lesson after school.   a.m.   p.m.

Brush your teeth before school.   a.m.   p.m.

Eat breakfast at 6:45.   a.m.   p.m.

14. Draw lines to match the time on each clock in the first row to the same time shown in the second row.

4:30   5:15   4:45   5:30

Name _____

The Toy Store

Terry's family owns a toy store.
These are some of the things
that they sell.

$14 $21 $1 38¢

1. Lorna paid for a box of crayons
with 6 coins.
Ken paid for a box of crayons
with 7 coins.
Draw the coins that each of them used.

Lorna's 6 coins	Ken's 7 coins

2. Kim goes to the toy store
with these coins.

Part A

What is the total value of the coins Kim
has? Explain how you know.

_____

_____

_____

Part B

How much more money does Kim need to
buy the book? Explain.

3. Kay's father buys a toy train at the toy store for $50.

Part A

Show five different ways that he could have paid $50. Use tally marks to complete the table.

Ways to Show $50			
$20 Bill	$10 Bill	$5 Bill	Total
			$50
			$50
			$50
			$50
			$50

Part B

Which way uses the least number of bills to make $50? Explain.

4. Ted walks to the toy store in the afternoon.

Part A

He starts walking at the time shown on the digital clock. Draw hands on the second clock to show the same time.

Is the time on the clocks above 3:35 a.m. or 3:35 p.m.? Explain how you know.

Part B

Ted gets to the store 10 minutes later. Write this time in two different ways.

Glossary

A

add

When you add, you join groups together.

$$3 + 4 = 7$$

addend

numbers that are added

$$2 + 5 = 7$$
addends

after

424 comes after 423.

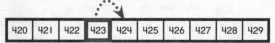

a.m.

clock time from midnight until noon

7:10 PM

angle

the corner shape formed by two sides that meet

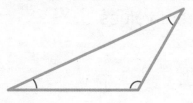

array

a group of objects set in equal rows and columns that forms a rectangle

B

bar diagram

a model for addition and subtraction that shows the parts and the whole

15

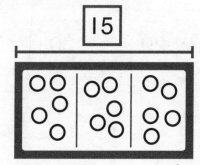

bar graph

A bar graph uses bars to show data.

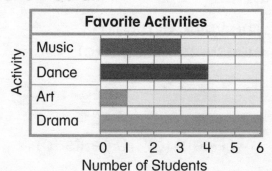

Favorite Activities

before

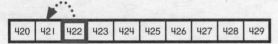

421 comes before 422.

break apart

You can break apart a number into its place value parts.

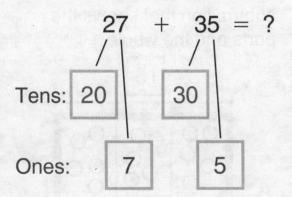

27 + 35 = ?

Tens: 20   30

Ones: 7   5

cents

The value of a coin is measured in cents (¢).

1 cent (¢)   10 cents (¢)

centimeter (cm)

a metric unit of length that is part of 1 meter

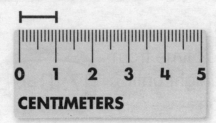

CENTIMETERS

coins

money that is made out of metal and that can have different values

1¢   5¢   10¢   25¢   50¢

column

objects in an array or data in a table that are shown up and down

← column

1	2	3	4	5
11	12	13	14	15
21	22	23	24	25
31	32	33	34	35

compare

When you compare numbers, you find out if a number is greater than, less than, or equal to another number.

147 $>$ 143

147 is greater than 143.

compatible numbers

numbers that are easy to add or subtract using mental math

8 + 2
20 + 7
53 + 10

compensation

a mental math strategy you can use to add or subtract

38 + 24 = ?
+2   −2

You add 2 to 38 to make 40. Then subtract 2 from 24 to get 22. 40 + 22 = 62. So, 38 + 24 = 62.

cone

a solid figure with a circle shaped base and a curved surface that meets at a point

cube

a solid figure with six faces that are matching squares

cylinder

a solid figure with two matching circle shaped bases

data

information you collect and can be shown in a table or graph

Favorite Fruit	
Apple	7
Peach	4
Orange	5

decrease

to become lesser in value

$$600 \longrightarrow 550$$

600 decreased by 50 is 550.

denominator

the number below the fraction bar in a fraction, which shows the total number of equal parts

$\frac{3}{4}$ ⟵ denominator

difference

the answer in a subtraction equation or problem

$$14 - 6 = 8$$

↑
difference

digits

Numbers are made up of 1 or more digits. 43 has 2 digits.

dime

10 cents or 10¢

division

an operation that tells how many equal groups there are or how many are in each group

$$12 \div 3 = 4$$

divided by

what you say to read a division symbol

$$18 \div 3 = 6$$

 divided by

dollar

One dollar equals 100¢.

dollar bills

paper money that can have different dollar values, such as $1, $5, $10, or $20

dollar sign

a symbol used to show that a number represents money

$$\$37$$

↑ dollar sign

doubles

addition facts that have two addends that are the same

$$4 + 4 = 8$$

↑ addend ↑ addend

edge

a line formed where two faces of a solid figure meet

 edge

eighths

When a whole is separated into 8 equal shares, the parts are called eighths.

equal groups

groups that have the same number of items or objects

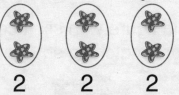

2   2   2

equal shares

parts of a whole that are the same size

All 4 shares are equal.

equals (=)

has the same value

$$36 = 36$$

36 is equal to 36.

equation

a math sentence that uses an equal sign (=) to show that the value on the left is equal to the value on the right

$$3 + ? = 7$$
$$14 - 6 = 8$$

estimate

When you estimate, you make a good guess.

This table is about 3 feet long.

even

a number that can be shown as a pair of cubes.

8 is even.

expanded form

a way of writing a number that shows the place value of each digit

$$400 + 60 + 3 = 463$$

face

a flat surface of a solid figure that does not roll

faces

fact family

a group of related addition and subtraction facts

$$2 + 4 = 6$$
$$4 + 2 = 6$$
$$6 - 2 = 4$$
$$6 - 4 = 2$$

factors

numbers that are multiplied together to give a product

$$7 \times 3 = 21$$

factors

flat surface

flat surfaces that are **NOT** faces

foot (ft)

a standard unit of length equal to 12 inches

fourths

When a whole is divided into 4 equal shares, the shares are called fourths.

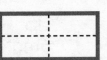

fraction

a number, such as $\frac{1}{2}$ or $\frac{3}{4}$, that names part of a whole or part of a set

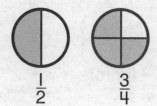

$\frac{1}{2}$ $\frac{3}{4}$

greater than (>)

has greater value

$$5 > 1$$

5 is greater than 1.

greatest

the number in a group with the largest value

35 47 58 61
greatest

greatest value

The coin that has the greatest value is the coin that is worth the most.

The quarter has the greatest value.

half-dollar

50 cents or 50¢

half past

30 minutes past the hour

It is half past 9.

halves (half)

When a whole is divided into 2 equal shares, the shares are called halves.

height

how tall an object is from bottom to top

heptagon

a polygon that has 7 sides

hexagon

a polygon that has 6 sides

hour

An hour is 60 minutes.

hundred

10 tens make 1 hundred.

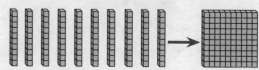

I

inch (in.)

a standard unit of length that is part of 1 foot

INCHES

increase

to become greater in value

550 ⟶ 600

550 increased by 50 is 600.

L

least

the number in a group with the smallest value

35 47 58 61
least

least value

The coin that has the least value is the coin that is worth the least.

The dime has the least value.

length

the distance from one end to the other end of an object

less than (<)

has less value

2 < 6

2 is less than 6.

line plot

A line plot uses dots above a number line to show data.

Lengths of Shells

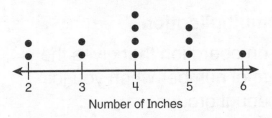

Number of Inches

M

Start at 23. Count on 2 tens. 33, 43

mental math

math you do in your head

23 + 20 = 43

meter (m)

a metric unit of length equal to 100 centimeters

A long step is about a meter.

minute

a standard length of time

There are 60 minutes in 1 hour.

multiplication

an operation that gives the total number when you join equal groups

$$3 \times 2 = 6$$

To multiply 3×2 means to add 2 three times.

$$2 + 2 + 2 = 6$$

near doubles

addition facts that have two addends that are close

$$4 + 5 = 9$$

↑ addend   ↑ addend

nearest centimeter

The whole number centimeter mark closest to the measure is the nearest centimeter.

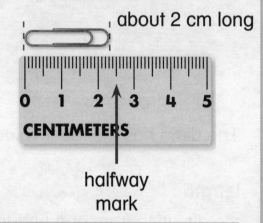

about 2 cm long

CENTIMETERS

halfway mark

nearest inch

The whole number inch mark closest to the measure is the nearest inch.

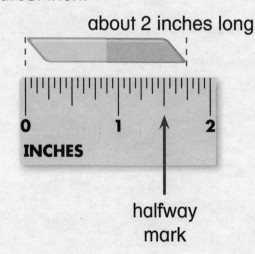

about 2 inches long

INCHES

halfway mark

next ten

the first ten greater than a number

30 is the next ten after 27.

nickel

5 cents or 5¢

nonagon

a polygon that has 9 sides

number line

a line that shows numbers in order from left to right

1 2 3 4 5 6 7 8 9 10

numerator

the number above the fraction bar in a fraction, which shows how many equal parts are described

$\frac{3}{4}$ ← numerator

octagon

a polygon that has 8 sides

odd

a number that can **NOT** be shown as pairs of cubes

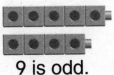

9 is odd.

ones

digits that shows how many ones are in a number

54 + 14 = 68
↑ ↑ ↑

open number line

An open number line is a tool that can help you add or subtract. It can begin at any number.

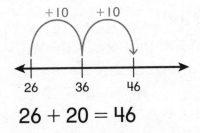

26 + 20 = 46

order

to place numbers from least to greatest or from greatest to least

27 72 107 117 171

least ↱   greatest ↱

parallelogram

a quadrilateral that has 4 sides and opposite sides parallel

part

a piece of a whole or of a number

2 and 3 are parts of 5.

partial sum

When you add numbers, the sum of one of the place values is called a partial sum.

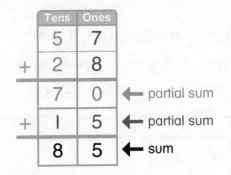

penny

I cent or I ¢

pentagon

a polygon that has 5 sides

picture graph

a graph that uses pictures to show data

Favorite Ball Games	
Baseball	⚇⚇
Soccer	⚇⚇⚇⚇⚇⚇⚇
Tennis	⚇⚇⚇⚇

Each ⚇ = I student

place-value chart

a chart matches each digit of a number with its place

Hundreds	Tens	Ones
3	4	8

plane shape

a flat shape

circle   rectangle   square   triangle

p.m.

clock time from noon until midnight

polygon

a closed plane shape with 3 or more sides

product

the answer to a multiplication problem

$$4 \times 2 = 8$$

product

pyramid

a solid figure with a base that is a polygon and faces that are triangles that meet in a point

Q

quadrilateral

a polygon that has 4 sides

quarter

25 cents or 25¢

quarter past

15 minutes after the hour

It is quarter past 4.

quarter to

15 minutes before the hour

It is quarter to 4.

R

rectangular prism

a solid figure with bases and faces that are rectangles

regroup

to name a number or part in a different way

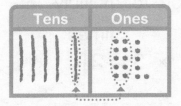

10 ones can be regrouped as 1 ten. 1 ten can be regrouped as 10 ones.

related

Addition facts and subtraction facts are related if they have the same numbers.

$$2 + 3 = 5$$
$$5 - 2 = 3$$

repeated addition

adding the same number repeatedly

$$3 + 3 + 3 + 3 = 12$$

right angle

an angle that forms a square corner

row

objects in an array or data in a table that are shown across

1	2	3	4	5
11	12	13	14	15
21	22	23	24	25
31	32	33	34	35

← row

 S

separate

to subtract or to take apart into two or more parts

$$5 - 2 = 3$$

side

a line segment that makes one part of a plane shape

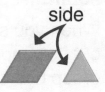
side

solid figure

a shape that has length, width, and height

These are all solid figures.

sphere

a solid figure that looks like a ball

standard form

a way to write a number using only digits

436

subtract

When you subtract, you find out how many are left or which group has more.

$$5 - 3 = 2$$

sum

the answer to an addition equation or problem

$$3 + 4 = 7$$

$$\begin{array}{r} 4 \\ + 3 \\ \hline 7 \end{array}$$

sum → 7

symbol

a picture or character that stands for something

The symbol will be ☖.
Each ☖ represents
1 student.

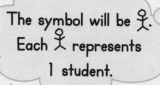

---

tally mark

a symbol used to keep track of each piece of information in an organized list

Ways to Show 30¢			
Quarter	Dime	Nickel	Total
I		I	30¢
	III		30¢
	II	II	30¢
	I	IIII	30¢
		⊮ I	30¢

tens

the digit that shows how many groups of ten are in a number

238

thirds

When a whole is divided into 3 equal shares, the shares are called thirds.

---

thousand

10 hundreds make 1 thousand.

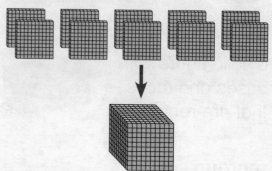

times

another word for multiply

times

$$7 \times 3 = 21$$

trapezoid

a polygon with 4 sides and one pair of sides are parallel

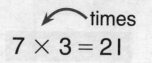

triangular prism

a solid figure that has two triangle shaped bases and three faces that have rectangle shapes.

unequal

Unequal parts are parts that are not equal.

5 unequal parts

unit

You can use different units to measure.

about 12 inches
about 1 foot

unit fraction

a fraction that reperesents one equal part of a whole or a set

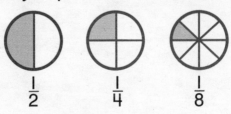

$\frac{1}{2}$ $\frac{1}{4}$ $\frac{1}{8}$

unknown

a symbol that stands for a number in an equation

$$34 + ? = 67$$

↑
unknown

vertices (vertex)

vertex

corner points where 2 sides of a polygon meet or where edges of a solid figure meet

whole

a single unit that can be divided into parts

The two halves make one whole circle.

width

the distance across an object

word form

a way to write a number using only words

The word form for 23 is twenty-three.

yard (yd)

a standard unit of length equal to 3 feet

A baseball bat is about a yard long.

enVisionmath 2.0

Photographs

Photo locators denoted as follows: Top (T), Center (C), Bottom (B), Left (L), Right (R), Background (Bkgd)